Spotlight on Wire

Twist • Fold • Hammer • Weave • Wrap

Melissa Cable

KB

KALMBACH BOOKS

Kalmbach Books
21027 Crossroads Circle
Waukesha, Wisconsin 53186
www.Kalmbach.com/Books

Step-by-step photography by the author. All other photography by Kalmbach Books.

Published in 2011
15 14 13 12 11   1 2 3 4 5

Manufactured in the United States of America

ISBN: 978-0-87116-437-7

Publisher's Cataloging-in-Publication Data

Cable, Melissa, 1970-
     Spotlight on wire : twist, fold, hammer, weave, wrap / Melissa Cable.

     p. : col. ill. ; cm.

     ISBN: 978-0-87116-437-7

     1. Wire jewelry–Handbooks, manuals, etc. 2. Wire jewelry–Patterns. 3. Jewelry making–Handbooks, manuals, etc. I. Title.

TT212 .C23 2011
739.27

TABLE OF CONTENTS

INTRODUCTION

For seven years, I was the lucky proprietor of beadclub bead store in Woodinville, Wash. To this day, my (and my employees') favorite class to teach was Wire 101. It was the most satisfying because, inevitably, nearly every student who took the class would have an "ah-ha" moment … the moment where desire and possibility meet, where skill and creativity intersect. At some point, even the student who had introduced herself to the class as the "least creative person I know" would say, "hey, I can do this … and it actually looks like something I would buy!" That enthusiasm is what fuels any teacher; it's addicting and always in demand.

It was no surprise or accident that I chose wire as the topic of my first book. Wire is a great medium for beginners and experienced artisans alike. For many, it serves as a first introduction to metal and to metalworking tools, and it paves the path to further metalwork. My desire is to do just that: Set you on a journey while giving you the skills you need to confidently choose your jewelry-making path. Therefore, rather than present a purely project-based book, you'll notice that each chapter in *Spotlight on Wire* focuses on working with wire in a different way: weaving and corrugating, texturing, and working with heavy wire, beading wire, and chain. You may be a beginner, or you may have tried some of this before. My goal is to "add to your toolbox" of skills and techniques, while also giving you an opportunity to complete fun projects that you can show off and be proud of.

Several of these projects were created by former employees and beadclub instructors Pam Brown and Corinna VanKleeck. Their years of teaching hundreds, if not thousands, of students to work with wire, combined with their creative and engineering minds, have resulted in gorgeous designs that support the skills this book aims at passing on to you.

The wire journey begins in Chapter 1 with weaving. You'll learn to capture beads in a free-form net (Captive Clusters and Urban Grace) or in a structured, patterned design (Forbidden Fruit). You'll have an opportunity to use wire as a way to cluster beads (Clustered Jewels and Woven Treasures), or create stand-alone components (Hanging Gardens and Jeweled Webs). In this chapter I'll share methods for choosing wire and how to avoid kinks when weaving wire, and introduce basic tools including dowels and metal punches.

Applying textures to wire is the basis of Chapter 2. Rather than focus on common methods such as hammering and stamping, I'll introduce an innovative technique that lets you apply intricate texture to metal at a fraction of the price that it would normally cost to achieve such a look. It's also the first foray beyond round wire. The two pendant and three bracelet projects in this chapter use strip wire. I'll discuss the merits of this type of wire at the start of the chapter, as well as the benefits of owning a good pair of metal shears.

In Chapter 3, you'll learn to corrugate, or create ripples in, round wire and strip wire with a tool called a tube wringer. My personal favorite project, Berry Vines, not only teaches you to corrugate and embellish round wire, but allows you an opportunity to customize your design with a framed pendant. You'll also learn to corrugate wire using pliers when you make the Rippled Bangle.

Chapter 4 introduces heavy wire. Larger gauges have their own considerations and some are addressed here, such as how to avoid marring heavy wire while working with it and what tools are handy to use with heavier gauges. Heavy wire can stand on its own in designs, so you'll learn to create spiraled components

As an instructor, Wire 101 was the most satisfying class to teach because, inevitably, nearly every student who took the class would have an "ah-ha" moment…the moment where desire and possibility meet, where skill and creativity intersect.

(Bejeweled Spirals and Heavy Metal), charm holders (Charming Story), chains (Sam's Chain), and lampworked bead-embellished cuffs (Andromeda Cuff).

Alternative wires, such as beading wire, and complementary materials, including chain, are the focus of Chapter 5. A series of earrings introduce a method for combining beading wire and chain. The pièce de résistance however, is the Arabian Cuff —featuring more than 100 dangling chain pieces in a cuff with incredible movement and texture. The final piece in this chapter was inspired by another instructor, Cristina Hererra, who liked to work with wire and it is in her memory that I used one of her innovative techniques to pair chain and wire.

There is a lot of ground to cover, so to make your journey easier, I've provided a road map along the way, with signs that let you know what basic skills you need to know to complete any project. These basics are outlined in Chapter 6 and include instruction on findings, finishes, cords, and basic techniques, such as wire-wrapping and crimping with pliers. Within these basics, we've discussed the tools that are used to accomplish these skills, such as hammers, bench blocks, burs, butane torches, and more. If you are new to wirework, it might be worth reviewing Chapter 6 before beginning your first project. Otherwise, use the handy icons that accompany each project to guide you to the required basic techniques.

No matter how you approach this book, whether you review the basics first, progress chapter by chapter, or jump right in to your favorite project, you're bound to enjoy the versatility, ease, and satisfaction of working with wire. And, you never know what direction it will take you. I certainly could not have predicted it would take me on this adventure of sharing my love of the art with students nationwide. So as you begin your journey, don't simply look straight down the road as you go … look side to side and up and down. You never know—you too may discover a brand-new path with wire.

Melissa Cable

Project by Corinna VanKleeck

HOW TO USE THIS BOOK

Each project is labeled with icons that identify the basic skills required to complete the project. These basics are outlined in Chapter 6. Within these basics, tools are identified as well, such as hammers, steel bench blocks, burs, butane torches, and more. If you are new to wirework, it might be worth reviewing the basics before beginning your first project. Otherwise, use the handy icons to guide you.

In addition to the Spotlight on Basics featured in Chapter 6, specific tips, techniques, and tools are identified within each chapter. Many of these topics are applicable to projects throughout the book, so be sure to revisit them periodically to review the information provided.

Basics

Spotlight: Tips and Techniques

Spotlight: Tools

Chapter 1 • Woven Wire

All woven wire projects have one thing in common: their intricate structures appear harder to achieve than they actually are, making them the show-stoppers among your jewelry collection. They can be structured or free-form, fancy or casual. They can spotlight a beautiful bead by framing it, or allow the wire to be the star. Woven wire projects often have the appearance of texture difficult to achieve with any other technique. This texture makes these projects a natural choice for patinas and areas of highlights and lowlights after polishing. Whatever type of woven wire projects you choose, your creations will likely become some of your favorites.

SPOTLIGHT
Tips and Techniques

Choosing Wire

You first choice is between dead-soft, half-hard, or full-hard wire. Purpose is the deciding factor when choosing wire. For most wire-woven projects, the purpose will be either framing wire or weaving wire.

Since, in nearly all cases, framing wire is the wire that creates the structure and support for the delicate weaving that surrounds it, half-hard wire is most appropriate for framing. Weaving wire needs the flexibility to wind its way around the frame, making dead-soft wire the optimal choice.

What do the terms half-hard, dead-soft or full-hard wire mean? When wire is created, it's drawn through a tool called a draw plate. A draw plate sizes the wire down to the gauge intended for that wire. How hard the wire gets in this process is determined by how many times the wire goes through the draw plate. Traditionally, dead-soft wire has gone through a draw plate only once, making it very pliable and easy to manipulate. Half-hard wire has passed through a draw plate several times, and as a result, it's harder. Working with it is slightly more difficult, but it holds shapes much better than its dead-soft counterpart. Finally, full-hard wire, as you can guess, has made even more passes through a draw plate, making it very hard, and often extremely difficult to reshape because it tends to want to spring back to its original form.

There is one other option, specifically when it comes to silver wire. Fine silver wire is 99.9% pure silver, making it softer than its counterpart sterling silver, which is an alloy made up of 92.5% silver and 7.5% of another metal, most often copper. It is for this reason that fine silver can often serve as a substitute when you need dead-soft wire.

Don't Get Kinky

One of the biggest challenges with woven-wire projects is to prevent the wire from kinking as you weave it. Kinks not only create unattractive blemishes, they cause weak points and are the main source of wire breaks. Each time the wire kinks, it becomes harder in that area. As the wire gets harder, it become more brittle, eventually to the point that it breaks.

To avoid kinks, concentrate on always keeping a smooth rounded loop as you pull the wire through or around the frame wire. Don't allow the loop to pass over itself and create a teardrop shape. Instead, it should lay like a gentle "U" turn. To help keep the wire from flipping and passing over itself, insert an awl in the "U" and allow the wire to pull against it as you tighten it into the weave. Artist Loren Damewood, a master at creating intricate knots and weaves with wire, told me long ago that a chopstick in your toolkit was your best friend … and to this day, I always have one on hand to help me prevent kinks in my woven wirework.

SPOTLIGHT Tools

Dowels

Throughout the book, you will find many projects that call for dowels of certain sizes. Sometimes a dowel is used to create a circular form; other times it's used as a place holder to keep a consistent space between two wires. The use and the wire type will determine what type of dowel you should choose.

When creating simple circular forms with light- to medium-gauge wires, such as the webs in the Jeweled Webs project, wooden dowels are an ideal choice. They are easy to source and come in a variety of sizes. It is important to not wrap the wire too tightly around a wooden dowel, as the wire can eat into the wood and become stuck.

When using a dowel to help keep consistent spacing, such as in the Forbidden Fruit project, it's best to use a metal dowel. Because wooden dowels have some give, they do not have the ability to hold the space as precisely as metal dowels.

Finally, when creating round shapes with heavier gauge wires, you may want to consider substituting dowels with stepped pliers sold as the brand "Wrap N Tap." Read more about this in Chapter 4.

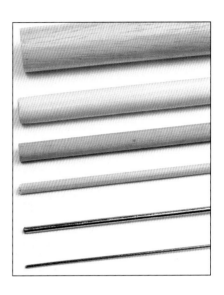

Metal Hole Punches

Punches, perhaps more than any other tool, open up the possibilities for hobbyists who want to work with metal. Instead of dealing with drills, we can now turn to metal hole-punch pliers and tools to pierce quick holes into metal. Making holes easily enhances This is not only handy to create original pieces, but also to turn a charm into a link by adding another hole on the opposite end, to add multiple holes on the bottom of a charm for dangling bead embellishments, or to enlarge a hole that might be too small. While there are many types of metal hole-punch tools, I will focus on two of them here: punch pliers and screw punches.

Metal hole-punch pliers come in a variety of shapes and sizes that can punch up to 18-gauge copper. Most common are round hole punches that make 1.25 mm and 1.8 mm holes (these are just slightly smaller than 16- and 13-gauge wire). In recent years, pliers have been made that punch oval and square holes. I find these two punches especially useful when working with strip wire. For example, by punching square holes directly next to each other, you can create a slot wide enough to accommodate a piece of strip wire. This is great when connecting pieces of strip wire together, or for creating a strip-wire bail. These pliers last a long time because the peg is replaceable. And if you are like me, you will wear them out quickly as you push the boundaries of what you should be punching!

You also can use a screw-style metal hole punch. The peg sizes are 1.6 mm and 2.3 mm, equivalent to 14- and 11-gauge wire. While this tool may be a little slower to use, and the hole placement is limited to the depth of the punch's throat, I find that the screw-style punches give a clean hole with little "splay" coming out of the back. This means that there is less clean up, or filing, after you punch a hole. Because of this, I often use this punch when I am working on a project that has a lot of holes, such as the Rippled Bangle in Chapter 3.

CLUSTERED JEWELS

Large mother-of-pearl rectangular focal beads were the original inspiration for these shimmering pendants, but any flat bead makes an interesting canvas for a jeweled cluster. This project is a great way to use your bead soup—all those leftover single beads that have no home but still want to be loved.

Materials
- 30 x 40 mm flat bead or shell
- **30–40** assorted 3–6 mm beads
- 3-in. (76 mm) 22-gauge headpin
- bail (optional)
- 2½ ft. (76.2 cm) 28-gauge craft wire

Tools
- roundnose pliers
- chainnose pliers
- wire cutters

Recommended Cord: SK

BY MELISSA CABLE

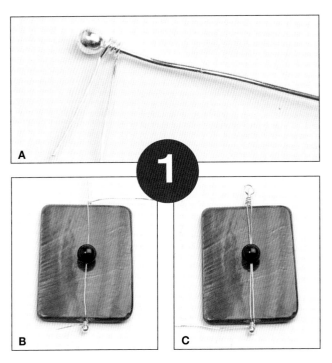

Step 1: Create the base wire

A Make three wraps with the 28-gauge wire at the bottom of the headpin, leaving a short tail. Wrap from the bottom up.

B String the shell onto the headpin. String a larger-hole bead onto the 28-gauge wire, bring the wire across the face of the shell, and make three wraps around the headpin directly above the shell. Center the bead.

C Make a wrapped loop on the headpin above the shell (if you are using a bail, connect the loop to the bail before you complete the wraps). Bring the wire back down through the bead, and wrap it around the bottom of the headpin once. Trim the tail from Step 1A. The two wires across the shell face are your base wire.

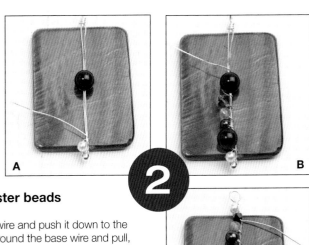

Step 2: String the cluster beads

A String a cluster bead onto the wire and push it down to the shell. String the wire under and around the base wire and pull, making sure the bead is tight against the base wire and the holes are horizontal. (If the bead lies vertically, the hole faces up and the wire is exposed.)

B Repeat Step 2A, placing beads next to each other along the base wire. When you reach the bead at the center of the base wire, go around the bead then under and around the base wire without adding another cluster bead. This will lock the center bead in place.

C Continue adding beads until you reach the wrapped loop. Your beads may or may not be to one side of the wire. Either way is fine. Wrap the wire 1^1/$_2$ times around the wrapped loop until the wire is at the back of the shell. Pull the wire through the wrapped loop from the back to front. Add another bead. Go under and around the base wire to secure the bead. This bead hides the wire wrap and keeps the shell from spinning on the headpin.

Step 3: Add the remaining beads

A Go back down the base wire, filling in the other side with beads.

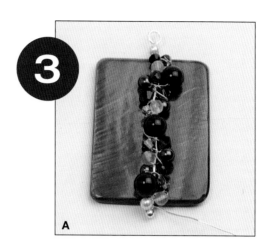

Once you reach the bottom, wrap the wire once around the bottom of the headpin, turn around, and head up the base wire again.

On this pass, randomly add beads where you need to hide exposed wire, add a color/texture, or fill a gap. You can then choose whether you want to make another pass down the shell. You can add more than one bead at a time (especially 3 mm beads) to make the cluster wider.

After your last pass of cluster beads, wrap the wire under the cluster and around the headpin (top or bottom, depending on number of passes) 2–3 times to secure it. Trim.

Hints

If your cluster has loose beads, or beads lay vertically exposing the wire coming out of their hole, twist the bead a half turn to tighten or realign it. Be sure not to twist it more than a half turn or it may snap the wire.

If you break a wire, simply back out of the last bead, and wrap that wire around the base wire twice to secure it. Then, starting on a different place on the base, wrap a new wire around the base twice before continuing with your cluster.

Create a bracelet in the same manner by first stringing all of your beads onto your beading wire, leaving room for them to slide. Then, pass a 28-gauge wire through a bead, center it, pass both wires across the face of the bead and secure both ends by wrapping them once around the beading wire. Using both wires, continue adding decorative beads in the same manner as the pendant.

CAPTIVE CLUSTERS

A beautiful flower arrangement in a vase filled with glass nuggets was the impetus for this project. Once the flowers faded, I became obsessed with finding ways to incorporate the nuggets into my jewelry. While these are quite nice set on metal disks, using a washer is even better: The hole in the center allows light to shine through the nugget, making the glass glow.

You can find copper, brass, and steel washers at your local hardware store, although you may be unable to use your hole-punch pliers to pierce thicker washers. I prefer to use 24-gauge sterling silver washers, which are available through many jewelry-supply companies.

HM PT

Materials
- 1 in. (25.5 mm) metal washer or disk
- 15 mm flat-back glass nugget
- **12** 3 mm beads
- 4 ft. (1.22 m) 26-gauge wire, dead-soft
- 4 in. (10.2 cm) 18-gauge craft wire

Tools
- roundnose pliers
- 1.8 mm hole-punch pliers (or screw punch for thicker washers)
- wire cutters
- chasing hammer
- steel bench block
- fine-point marker

Recommended Cord: SD

BY MELISSA CABLE

Step 1: Prepare the washer

Create a hammered finish of your choice on the washer (p. 105).

A Center the glass nugget on the washer and trace with a fine-point marker.

B Picture a clock dial. Punch a hole at 6 o'clock and a second hole at 12 o'clock. Then, punch a hole at 3 o'clock and a hole at 9 o'clock.

C Now, punch two holes between each set of holes until you have 12 holes total. Use rubbing alcohol to remove any excess marker.

Step 2: Create a bail

Tip If you will be antiquing your piece, consider applying the patina on the metal disk and wire at this point. It will be easier to polish.

A Coil 1 ft. (30.5 cm) of 26-gauge wire tightly around the 18-gauge craft wire until you have a coiled tube. Remove the coil.

Cut the coil to the desired length for the bail. String and center the coil on 3 ft. (91.4 cm) of 26-gauge wire.

B Pick a hole on the washer. String one end of the 26-gauge wire through the front of the hole and one through the back, pulling tightly until you form a looped bail.

C From the back of the washer, string the wire end through an adjacent hole on the right. From the front of the washer, string the other wire end through an adjacent hole on the left.

D String the wire at the back of the washer back through the center hole. Wrap both wires around the base of the bail once.

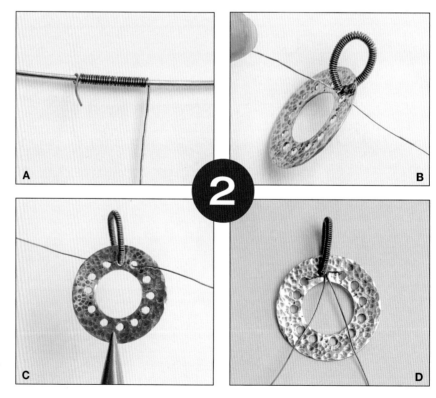

Step 3: Cage the glass nugget

Using your thumb, hold the glass nugget in the center of the washer. This will be difficult at first, but after a few passes with the wire, it will stay in place. Just make sure it stays centered.

A String a bead on each wire. Pull one wire across the nugget, down through a hole on the other side, and back up through an adjacent hole. Repeat with the other wire, going down through a different hole.

B Continue adding a bead and stringing the wire across the face of the nugget through another hole on the other side. Keep pushing the beads onto the nugget; don't let them sink down and lay on top of the hole.

Continue until all holes are connected on the back, creating a sewn effect. You can stop earlier if the nugget starts to become too covered by wire and beads.

Wrap the remaining wires between two adjacent holes once, trim to ⅛ in. (3 mm) and push the end under the glass nugget.

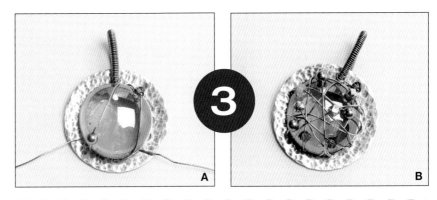

Hints

After pulling the wire through the hole tightly, create a 90-degree bend in the wire just below the hole to keep it from slipping back up through the hole as you string it through the adjacent hole. Be sure not to kink the wire; string it up and down through the holes slowly and carefully.

Avoid stringing the wire in a pattern, or you will have a stack of intersecting wires in the center of the nugget. Sometimes go straight across the top of the nugget, other times, go across the side, etc.

This is also a beautiful project for small tiles and other glass objects.

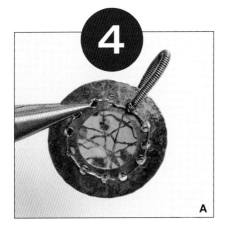

Step 4: Tighten the wires and beads

A Flatten the stitches in the back using chainnose pliers. To tighten the entire wire cage and keep the beads positioned where you want them, use roundnose pliers to place kinks in the wire.

HANGING GARDENS

As with the best creative endeavors, this pendant came to life as one project but quickly transformed into another as I became captivated by the movement achieved by cascading pearls and crystals from the bottom of the woven structure. Wire-wrap this pendant onto a convertible chain so you can wear it long or short (p. 108).

(p. 108).

BL **WW** **JR** **PT**

Materials
- **16–20** assorted 3–5 mm beads
- **4** 10–20 mm branch, leaf, or other charms
- **3** 15 mm tube or coil beads (optional)
- **5** mm ID 18-gauge jump ring,
- **6–8** 2½ mm ID 20-gauge jump rings (other sizes will work)
- **1** in. (25.5 mm) small cable chain
- **16–20** 26-gauge 1-in. headpins
- **3** 24-gauge 1½-in. (38 mm) headpins
- **7** ft. (2.13 m) 22-gauge wire, dead-soft
- **3** in. (76 mm) 20-gauge wire
- **1** ft. (30.5 cm) 16-gauge wire

Tools
- roundnose pliers
- chainnose pliers
- wire cutters
- **2** wide craft sticks
- 24-gauge or smaller craft wire
- 12 mm dowel

Recommended Cord: CH

BY MELISSA CABLE

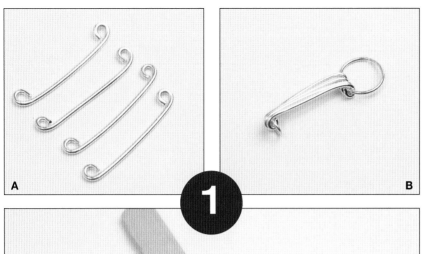

A

B

1

C

Step 1: Create the frame

Cut the 16-gauge wire into four 1¾-in. (44 mm) pieces. These are the stakes.

A Make a 3 mm loop at each end of each wire. (The wires will end up being 1¼-in./32 mm long once the loops are done.)

Using a 12 mm dowel, create a 16-gauge jump ring with the remaining 16-gauge wire.

B Open the 12 mm jump ring and string the loops on one end of the wires from A, making sure they are all facing the same direction. Close the jump ring. String the loops on the other end of the wires onto the 5 mm jump ring. This is the frame.

C Place craft sticks, width trimmed as needed, between the stakes and secure them with craft wire. This will help hold the shape of the piece until the woven wire is enough to hold it alone.

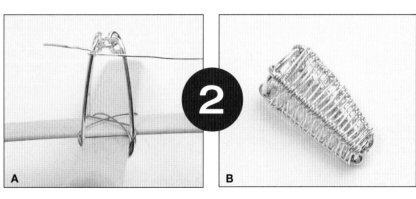

2

A

B

Step 2: Create horizontal weavers

A Cut a 3-ft. (91.4 cm) length of 22-gauge wire. Wrap one end around a stake so the wire is coming over the top of the stake. Pull the wire across and in front of the next stake, and wrap it around the stake.

B Repeat Step 2A until you have woven all the way down the frame. When you are finished, simply trim the wire after the last full wrap around a stake. Remove the craft sticks.

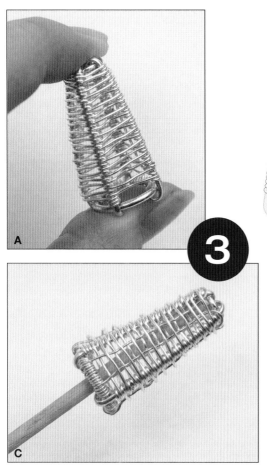

Step 3: Create vertical weavers

A Using round or chainnose pliers, push every other weaver in toward the inside of the frame.

B With one woven side facing you, start wrapping 1 ft. (30.5 cm). of 22-gauge wire away from you and to the right on the last third of the bottom jump ring **(1)**. When you reach the stake, continue around it, wrapping one third of the next section **(2)**. String the wire up between the weavers that are pulled straight and those that are pushed in **(3)**. Once you reach the top, cross over the stake to the left and string your wire down through the weavers on this panel **(4)**. Wrap wire toward you and to the left around the bottom jump ring until you have only a third of the jump ring still exposed **(5)**.

Repeat Step B until all sides have two vertical weavers.

C Using a dowel or pencil, come in from the inside of the frame and push the horizontal weavers back to lock the vertical weavers in place.

D Attach charms, such as the branch ones as shown, as desired to the sides of the frame.

Optional: Add patina and polish the piece at this time, remembering to use antiqued wire, chain, and jump rings in the next step.

Step 4: Add beads

A Wire-wrap beads as desired. Place 2–3 beads on each of the 2.5 mm ID jump rings and attach each ring to a chain link starting from the bottom of the chain. Adjust the cluster as desired by moving around beads and jump rings.

Wire-wrap a 3-in. (76 mm) piece of 20-gauge wire to the end of the chain and pull it through the top of the woven cone. You may need to place a bead on the wire above the chain to prevent the beads from pulling too high into the cone.

B Make a wrapped loop with the wire to serve as a bail. Wire-wrap to a toggle if using convertible chain (p. 108).

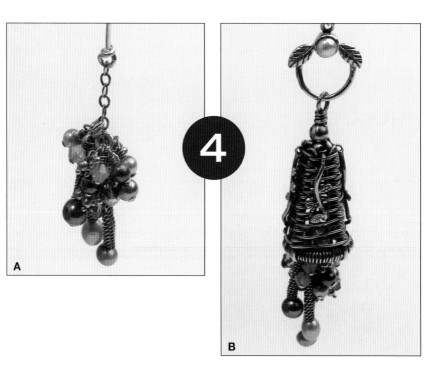

FORBIDDEN FRUIT

BL **WW** **JR**

Materials
- 25 x 18 mm flat oval bead
- 4 mm bicone crystal
- **2** 4 mm ID, 18-gauge jump rings
- 3 in. (76 mm) headpin
- 7 in. (17.8 cm) 18-gauge wire
- 2½ ft. (76.2 cm) 24-gauge wire, dead-soft
- 3 in. (76 mm) 14-gauge wire (or 15 mm ID, 14-gauge jump ring; other sizes will work)

Tools
- roundnose pliers
- chainnose pliers
- wire cutters
- small vice
- 15 mm wooden dowel
- ⅛ in. (3 mm) metal dowel
- painter's tape

Recommended Cord:
KD, CH (see hint)

This design can be made with a flat coin or oval bead of any size. (The cage shifts on rectangle and square beads.) The combination of the large red stone with the jump rings that flared out just perfectly, like leaves, gives the appearance of a caged apple. Hence the name: Forbidden Fruit.

BY MELISSA CABLE

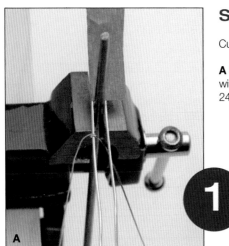

Step 1: Create the frame

Cut the 18-gauge wire into two 3½-in. (89 mm) pieces.

A Secure the metal dowel (standing straight up) in a small vice. Place a piece of 18-gauge wire on each side of the metal dowel and tape the top of the wires together. Center the 24-gauge wire on top of the left-hand frame wire and wrap it once.

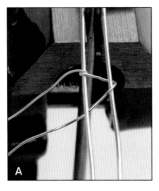
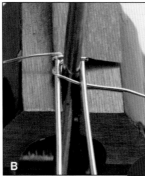
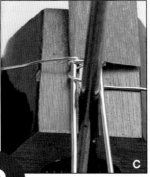

Step 2: Weave the wire

In this step, leave the frame on the dowel as you weave to maintain consistent spacing and tension throughout the weave.

A Pull the right-hand weaving wire across to the right-hand frame wire, go under and over the frame and cross back over to the left-hand wire frame, going under.

B Lift the entire frame off the dowel and place it back on the dowel so the dowel is in front of the weave you just made. Pull the weaving wire tightly as you push back against the weave you just made. Pass the wire over the left-hand frame wire, pass in front of the dowel going across the gap, and go under the right-hand frame wire.

C Once again, lift up the entire piece and place it back on the dowel so the dowel is in front of the weave you just made. Pull the weaving wire tightly so the weave you made slides up to the previous weave.

D Pass the wire over the right-hand frame wire, pass in front of the dowel going across the gap, and go under the left-hand frame wire.

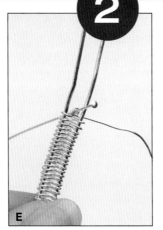

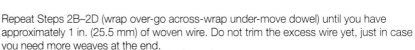

Repeat Steps 2B–2D (wrap over-go across-wrap under-move dowel) until you have approximately 1 in. (25.5 mm) of woven wire. Do not trim the excess wire yet, just in case you need more weaves at the end.

E Remove the frame from the dowel. Remove the tape, place tape on the other end and push the woven wire down to the tape. The second half of the weaving wire will now be toward the center point of the frame wire. Center the headpin between the frame wires and wrap the new weaving wire around it once.

F Remove the headpin, place the frame on the dowel so the previously woven section of wire is behind the dowel and repeat Step 2D. Remove the tape.

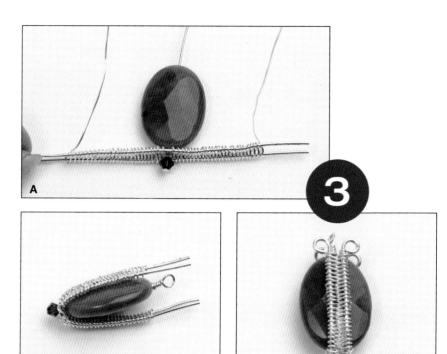

Step 3: Assemble

A String the 4 mm bicone crystal on the headpin. String the headpin into the hole on the woven frame. String the oval bead onto the headpin.

B Make a 3 mm wrapped loop on the headpin. Bend the woven frame in half. Check to see that the weave ends at the top of the bead on both sides. If it's too short, do a few more woven wraps. If it's too long, unweave a few passes. When it is just right, wrap the end of the weaving wire around the frame once before trimming.

C Trim the frame wires to ¼ in. (6.5 mm). Create a 4 mm loop on the end of each wire, rolling toward the outside of the bead. Make sure the loops sit just above the edge of the bead.

D Place a jump ring between the back and front loops on each side of the frame. If it's too tight, simply use a larger jump ring. If it's too loose and does not pull the frame loops toward each other, use a smaller jump ring. Make a 14-gauge jump ring using the 15 mm dowel. String the jump ring through the two jump rings and the wrapped loop on the headpin.

Hints

This is another design that works great hanging from a toggle, allowing you to wear it long or short (p. 108). The toggle takes the place of the 15 mm, 14-gauge jump ring. To accomplish this, be sure to wire-wrap the toggle into the loop you make on the headpin and then string the toggle into the jump rings when connecting the frame loops.

This design also works with 26-gauge weaving wire; you will need approximately 1½ times the amount of the 24-gauge wire, and it will take considerably longer as there will be more weaving.

JEWELED WEBS

Donuts can sometimes present a design challenge. Caging them in their own frame is one solution and will hopefully lead you to many new display ideas.

Materials
- 25 mm donut
- **35** 4–5 mm beads (as shown, 5 mm rondelles)
- **35** 3–4 mm beads (as shown, 3 mm bicone crystals)
- **8** 6 mm ID, 18-gauge jump rings
- 1 ft. (30.5 cm) chain
- 9½ ft. 22-gauge wire
- 7 ft. (2.13 m) 24-gauge wire

Tools
- roundnose pliers
- chainnose pliers
- wire cutters
- 10 mm dowel
- 13 mm dowel
- 20 mm dowel
- 30 mm dowel

BY PAM BROWN

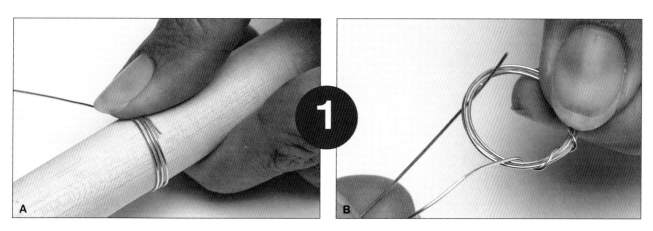

Step 1: Create the wire links

A Wrap one end of an 16-in. (40.6 cm) piece of 22-gauge wire around a 20 mm dowel three times. Remove the wraps from the dowel. If desired, hand shape the links into ovals before Step 1B.

B Wrap the long tail of the wire along the circle you just created. Once you have gone all the way around, tightly wrap the end of the wire around the circle to secure it. Be sure the first wrap is tight and secures the cut end of the wire on the circle.

Repeat Step 1A and 1B until you have two large links. Then, create three medium links by using 10 in. (25.4 cm) of 22-gauge wire on a 13 mm dowel, two small links by using 8 in. (40.6 cm) of 22-gauge wire on a 10 mm dowel, and the pendant link using 22 in. (55.9 cm) of 22-gauge wire on a 30 mm dowel.

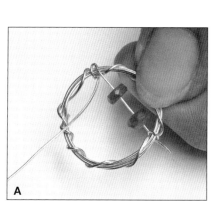
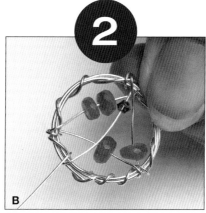
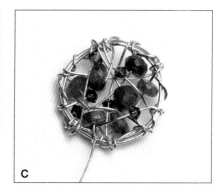
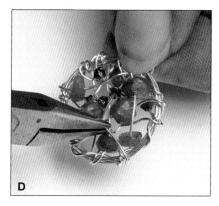

Step 2: Embellish the links

A Cut an 18-in. (45.7 cm) piece of 24-gauge wire. Secure it to a large link with one full wrap.

B String 1–2 beads and wrap the wire across the link at any angle. If the wire is coming from under the link, wrap it over the other side. Always alternate wrapping over and under so the links are not one sided.

C Continue wrapping until approximately 12 beads are secured. Secure wire with one or two tight wraps around the base circle. Repeat with remaining large links. Embellish the medium links in the same manner by using 1 ft. (30.5 cm) of 24-gauge wire and eight beads, and the small links by using 6 in. (15.2 cm) of 24-gauge wire and five beads.

D Create kinks in the wires to add more interest and to lock the beads into place. To do this, use chainnose pliers to gently grab the wire and twist a quarter turn.

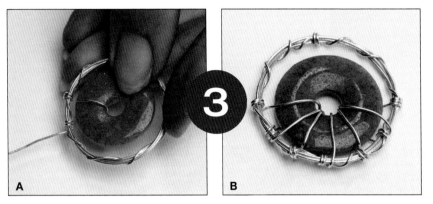

Step 3: Create the pendant

A Cut a 1-ft. piece of 22-gauge wire. Secure to the 30 mm link by wrapping tightly twice around the edge. Center the donut in the wire circle and, while holding it in place, wrap the wire over the front and through the center hole. Continue over the back edge of the donut and wrap two full times around the wire link.

B Cross back over the front of the donut, through the hole, and to the back of the donut. Go across the donut and secure twice around the wire frame.

Continue repeating 3B until you have a total of six strips of wire over the front and back of the bead. Be sure with each wrap you move across the wire frame to leave a space of about ¼ in. (6.5 mm) between wraps. Secure the wire end around the frame and trim. To secure the donut and add interest, use chainnose pliers to create kinks to every other wire laying across the donut.

Step 4: Assemble the necklace

A Connect a small link to a medium link with a 6 mm jump ring. Connect a large link to the medium link with a 6 mm jump ring. Repeat on the other side.

B Connect a medium link to the bottom of the donut pendant, slightly shaping it in an oval if desired.

Attach the pendant to the sections you attached together in Step 4A, using 6 mm jump rings to attach each large link and a third jump ring connecting the 6 mm jump rings together to hold the pendant centered.

Attach chain to each side of the necklace to achieve your desired length. An S-clasp is a great choice for this necklace as it will make it adjustable (p. 102).

project
alternate

CRYSTAL TORNADO

Materials
- 30 mm lampworked disk
- **9** 4 mm bicone crystals
- 2¼ ft. (38.1 cm) 22-gauge wire
- 2 ft. (61.0 cm) 24-gauge wire

Donuts or disks with small holes, such as a lampworked disk, require a slightly different treatment since it is usually impossible to fit multiple passes of 22-gauge wire through a smaller hole. Here is an alternative pendant for this necklace that makes a beautiful lampworked disk the star.

Project by Pam Brown

Step 1: Create and embellish the frame

A Wrap the 22-gauge wire four times around a 35 mm dowel. Remove the circle from the dowel and carefully form it into a teardrop shape. Wrap the wire tail around the teardrop link to secure it and end the wire by wrapping once tightly around the base, just as you did in Step 1 of the main project (p. 23).

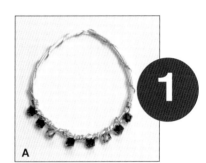

Cut a 14-in. (35.6 cm) piece of 24-gauge wire and wrap it twice around the link, about one third of the way from the bottom. Add a bicone and secure it by wrapping the wire twice around the base.

Continue adding bicones until they are centered evenly on the bottom third of the base, with the end bicones aligning.

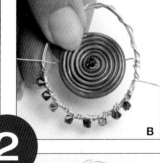

Step 2: Wire in the disk

A Cut a 10-in. (25.4 cm) piece of 24-gauge wire and string a bead to the center. Fold the sides down to secure the bead, and thread both ends through the center of the disk. Spread the two sides of the wire in opposite directions across the back of the disk.

B Holding the wire slightly above the midpoint of the disk (to prevent the disk from spinning), wrap each wire twice around the teardrop base and then once or twice about ½ in. (13 mm) down the base. Wrap twice around the base again and leave the excess wire.

C To end each wire, pull the wire across the back of the disk, wrap to the opposite wire (not to each other or the wire on its same side). Trim.

WOVEN TREASURES

Herringbone weave is a great way to frame beads. Whether to showcase a stand-alone bead or to, as in this case, make a more dramatic presentation, this weave can jazz up the simplest of beads.

Materials
- **5** 14 mm coin or lentil beads (other sizes will work) to fit 20-gauge wire
- **4–6** 6 mm beads to fit 20-gauge wire
- 1 ft. (30.5 cm) 20-gauge wire
- 6 ft. 22-gauge wire, dead soft

Tools
- roundnose pliers
- chainnose pliers
- wire cutters

BY PAM BROWN

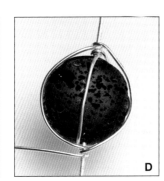

Step 1: The herringbone wrap

A Cut a 1 ft. (30.5 cm) piece of 20-gauge wire for the base wire. String and center a 14 mm bead. Cut a 15-in. (38.1 cm) length of 22-gauge wire and wrap the end once around the base wire, adjacent to the bead.

B Lay the 22-gauge wire on a slight diagonal across the face of the bead. Secure the wire to the base wire by wrapping once. If you do not want a zigzag on top of your bead, you can skip this step (I made half with and half without).

C Wrap the 22-gauge wire around the side of the bead and secure it to the base by wrapping over and around the wire. Always be sure to wrap over and around. Trim the starting tail.

D Repeat Step 1C, taking the wire to the other side of the bead.

E Continue weaving in this manner until you have four wraps on each side of the bead. Be sure to nestle the wire below the previous wires as you come around the side of the bead. Secure the wire with one full wrap and trim.

F If desired, create a zigzag on the face of the bead by gently turning the wire a quarter turn with chainnose pliers.

Step 2: Build the bracelet
String a 6 mm spacer bead on each side of the wrapped bead.

Continue adding herringbone wrapped beads on each side, for a total of five wrapped beads with a 6 mm spacer bead between each one. Depending on your desired length, you can add an additional spacer bead on the end. The wrapped beads slide easily on the base wire, so you can move them into position as you complete them.

You should have approximately 6¾ in. (17.1 cm) of wrapped beads and spacers, and 2½ in. (64 mm) of extra base wire on each side.

Step 3: The hook-and-eye closure

A Bend the wire 30 mm from the end. Use chainnose pliers to close the bend tightly.

B Roll the bent wire into a hook with roundnose pliers, wrap the wire end around the base wire twice, and trim.

Slide the beads to the hook, being careful not to stretch or compress the weaves. Begin to form the bracelet into a curve to accommodate any bead shifting before going to Step C.

C Make a wrapped loop on the other end of the base wire.

Carefully finish forming the bracelet into an oval, making sure there is enough tension between the hook and eye to keep the bangle closed.

To make a necklace, omit the hook and make a wrapped loop on each end of the wire, attaching 6 in. (15.2 cm) of chain to each end. Add decorative bead dangles and a lobster claw clasp.

URBAN GRACE

This necklace is not only a great unisex style, it also makes a wonderful hat band, and it can be adapted into a bracelet, anklet, or even earrings!

Materials
- 5–10 mm beads, strung length totalling 2½ in. (64 mm)
- 14 in. (35.6 cm) 4 mm braided leather cord
- 10 ft. (3.0 m) 22-gauge wire, dead-soft
- lobster claw clasp

Tools
- roundnose pliers
- chainnose pliers
- screw punch
- wire cutters
- electrical tape

BY CORINNA VANKLEECK

Step 1: Prepare the leather and the wire

If you are going to use antiqued wire, be sure to add patina and polish all your wire as desired before continuing (p. 106).

A Cut the leather into two equal pieces. If using braided leather cord, cut two 1-in. (25.5 mm) pieces of electrical tape, and then cut each piece lengthwise for a total of four pieces. Wrap a piece of tape around each leather end.

Slightly flatten the leather ends with chainnose pliers. Use the smallest hole on a screw punch to punch a hole ¼ in. (6.5 mm) from each end.

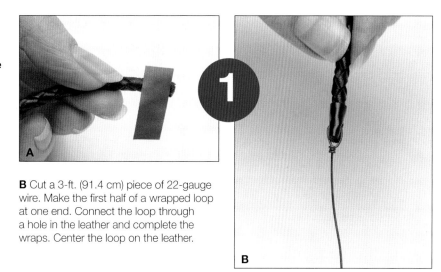

B Cut a 3-ft. (91.4 cm) piece of 22-gauge wire. Make the first half of a wrapped loop at one end. Connect the loop through a hole in the leather and complete the wraps. Center the loop on the leather.

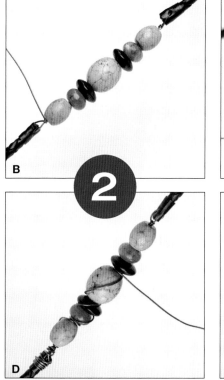

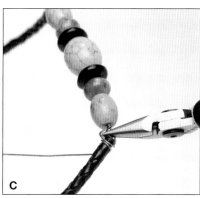

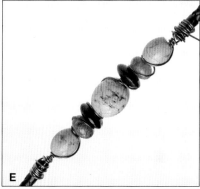

Step 2: Add beads

A String 2½ in. (64 mm) of 5–10 mm beads onto the wire. (More beads will get buried in the wire.)

B Wrap the wire to the end of a second piece of leather, following the technique in Step 1C.

C Hold onto the wire-wrap you just made with a pair of chainnose pliers and wrap the wire back around the leather for about ¼ in.

D Wrap the wire back toward the beads. Once you reach the beads, wrap the wire around the beads, nestling the wire between each bead.

E When you reach the other side of the beads, wrap the wire around the leather for about ¼ in., matching the wraps made in Step 2C. Trim and tuck any ends under.

Hints

Submerge the whole necklace in hot water to make the leather more supple. This will allow you to shape it and let it dry into the form you desire.

Use 24-gauge wire for a finer look, mix 22-gauge and 24-gauge for more texture, or use colored craft wire for more interest.

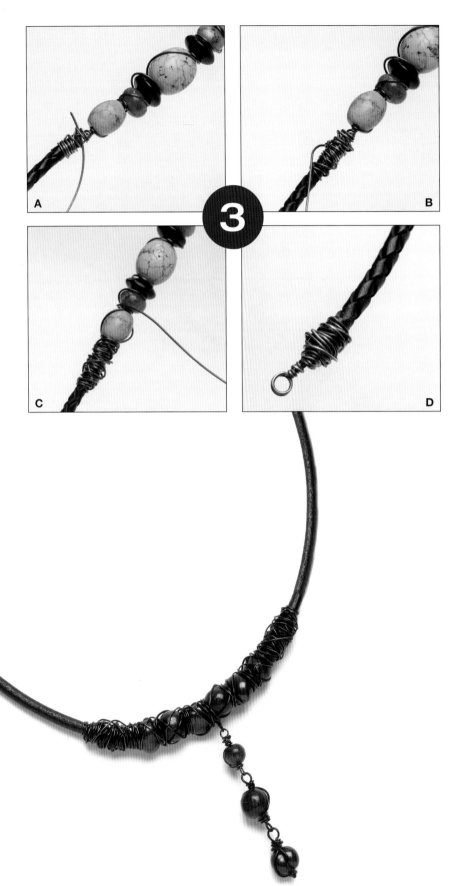

Step 3: Further embellish the beads

A Add a 3-ft. (91.4 cm) piece of 22-gauge wire by stringing it through a wrapped loop.

B Wrap back about ½ in. (13 mm) to cover any visible tape, and then wrap toward the beads again, creating a loosely wrapped coil. Tuck the tail of the new wire under the wraps.

C Wrap the wire over and around the beads again, as in Step 2D.

When you reach the other side, coil the remaining wire around the leather to make a coil that matches the wrap from Step 3B.

D Finish the ends by connecting 2 ft. (61.0 cm) of 22-gauge wire on each side of the leather (as in Step 1C). Create a wire wrapped loop directly below the wrap that is connecting the wire to the leather. Coil the remaining wire around the end of the leather. Be sure to add a clasp to one of the loops before you complete the wraps. For added durability, create a double loop on the side opposite from the clasp.

EARRINGS

Wire-wrap the ends of a 1-in. piece of leather cord as in Step 3D of the necklace.

String a bead on a headpin and make a wrapped loop, connecting it to one end of the cord. Complete the wraps on the loop.

Attach an earring wire to the other end. Repeat to make a second earring.

Chapter 2 • Textured Strip Wire

Now that we've successfully created overall texture on jewelry projects by weaving fine-gauge round wire, we'll take texture to a new level by embellishing the wire itself. To maximize the looks achieved with textures, we will explore using strip wire—a flat wire with a larger surface to showcase texture.

SPOTLIGHT
Tips and Techniques

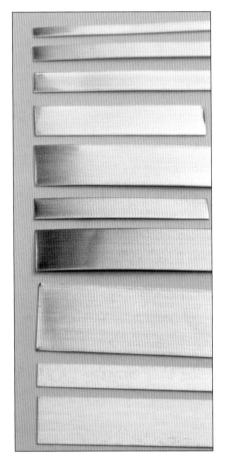

About strip wire

Strip wire is one of my favorite mediums. Its gauge, usually 26 or 24, is thin enough to manipulate, but thick enough to hold whatever shape I'm attempting. Its width, ranging from ⅛–1 in. (3–25.5 mm), is enough to show off all types of texturing, especially detailed textures achieved using brass plates and a rolling mill. Because of strip wire's consistent gauge and width, you can reliably use my poor-man's rolling mill method to create detailed textures without an expensive rolling mill. But first, lets talk more about strip wire.

Many jewelry hobbyists have not worked with strip wire because it seems to have limited availability. However, it's actually more readily available than you might think. Brass strip wire can easily be found in many hardware and hobbyist stores, most often in 26 gauge, ranging from ¼–1 in. (6.5–25.5 mm) wide by 1 ft. (30.5 cm) long. If you look carefully, you can sometimes find 3-ft. (91.4 cm) sections, which are great for the Rippled Bangle project in Chapter 3. Copper and sterling silver strip wire are carried by many of the leading jewelry catalogs and websites. Copper strip also can be sourced from companies that use it for interior and exterior architectural detailing.

There are two types of thinner-gauge strip wires that can come in handy. Copper restrip, used in stain glass work, is approximately 30 gauge. Silver bezel wire is usually 28 gauge. Although they are not thick enough to hold their shape on their own and the textures you apply often are not very deep, they make nice accents when you need a more flexible strip wire (as I did in the Dreaming of Pumpkins pendant). A list of suppliers that carry strip wire is provided in the resources section and you can always ask your local bead store if they'd be willing to order some in for you.

TIP
Local bead stores are a great resource for new materials, as they are always interested in knowing what supplies are up-and-coming in the world of jewelry making.

Since strip wire can be very sharp, run a fine-grain sandpaper along the edges before working with it. By slightly knocking off the harsh edge, you will greatly reduce the risk of a ghastly gash.

Poor-man's rolling mill

I absolutely love texture, and while I like the look created by textured hammers and metal stamps, I longed to achieve the effect of embossed or etched metal without expensive tools or messy chemicals. I set out to find a way to transfer brass texture plates onto strip wire. Brass texture plates come in dozens of designs, are inexpensive, and last a long time—a natural choice for texturing strip wire. While I had some success with taping the strip wire to the texture plate, placing it on a steel bench block, and hammering it, this was a loud, time-consuming, and clumsy process. The results weren't always consistent and over time, the plates became damaged and needed to be replaced more often.

And then I saw it—clamped to my craft table—my pasta machine, which had served me well in my brief encounter with polymer clay. I wondered, "if …?," and my mind began to wander. Well, two years and five broken pasta machines later, I can tell you with certainty what will work and what won't work when it comes to texturing metal using a hand-crank pasta machine and brass metal plates. First of all, it's only fair that I point out that these machines are not made to texture heavy metals. The manufacturer's directions recommend using only light metals, such as foils. However, I have found—using very specific guidelines—you can use a pasta machine to texture strip wire, and strip wire only. Believe me, I have experimented with wire, disks, jump rings, odd-shaped sheet metal … you name it. And over time, as I mentioned, I broke five machines in my quest to see just how far I could go. Just because something works once, doesn't mean it's going to work again.

There are many variables at play: how thick the texture plate is, its location in the pasta machine, the location of the metal on the texture plate, etc. But if you stick with the following guidelines, you'll not only have consistent results, you'll save yourself from breaking your pasta machine.

First, this method only works with copper and silver strip wire (brass strip is too hard to accept the texture). Second, don't go thicker than 24 gauge. Finally, use strip wire that is less than ½ in. (13 mm). If you stick with these three parameters, you'll achieve success every time.

Brass texture plates are generally 18 gauge and often come 2 in. (51 mm) wide and in varying lengths. I use pieces that are 3½ in. (89 mm) long, which are commonly sold by metal clay suppliers. To keep them in order, I number them, punch a hole in the corner and place them on shower rings. That way, when I use them, I can keep track of what texture I used in case I want to repeat the

look at a later date. I also use my metal shears to cut them into ½-in. strips that I use to create my own patchwork texture plates, as you will see later. I keep a stock of 26- and 24-gauge plain brass sheet in the same size as my texture plates.

To texture strip wire, sandwich it between a plain brass sheet and a texture plate. If the texture is deep, use 26-gauge plain sheet. If it's shallow, use 24-gauge sheet. If you have trouble holding the sheet without the strip falling out, tape the strip wire to the texture plate with painter's tape before sandwiching it between the sheets. Just remember, you've added thickness by using the tape, so you'll likely need to use the 26-gauge plain sheet to sandwich the metal. All pasta machine models are different, so you'll need to experiment a little. You want a setting that provides some resistance, but doesn't make you force the piece through. I use setting 4 or 5 on my machine, which has nine settings. Center the sandwich at the top of the pasta machine and push down gently as you turn the handle. As the metal comes out, gently guide it to one side of the pasta machine; that way, your two plates will have the same arc in them, making them go through the machine smoothly each time.

Yep, that's it! The texture should be transferred onto the metal. If it's not, or if the texture isn't deep enough to feel with your fingernail, you'll need to either change the pasta machine setting to move the rollers closer together, or use a thicker plain brass sheet to sandwich your metal. These textures especially pop when antiqued, so visit Chapter 6 and learn about how to blacken and polish metal.

To create a patchwork texture plate, lay ½-in. pieces of texture plate against each other on a piece of 1½ in. or wider painter's tape. Make sure there are no gaps between the plates, or your strip wire will have a deep gouge there and will likely break or will resist bending smoothly at that point. Have a piece of plain brass sheet available that is the same length as the patchwork of texture. Tape the strip wire to the patchwork, sandwich it with the plain sheet, and use the pasta machine as described above.

A few hints: only texture one piece of metal at a time. I find that if I put two pieces side by side, one textures better than the other one, which may not texture at all. Secondly, long pieces of strip wire may slightly arc sideways as they pass through the machine. Usually, these slight variations do not affect my design, but if you have a problem with the metal being misshapen, simply place it on its side on a metal steel bench block and gently tap it with a rawhide hammer.

SPOTLIGHT Tools

Metal shears

While strip wire can be cut with heavy-duty wire cutters, I prefer metal shears. They not only allow me to get a straight cut, they also allow me to cut rounded edges, reducing the amount of filing I might have to do. There are many types of metal shears out there, and I encourage you to try different kinds to find the best fit for you. When looking for a pair of shears, try to find one with thin blades, allowing you to do more detailed cuts. Also try to find a pair that has a longer blade, rather than a short tin-snip style blade. The longer blades allow for smoother cuts and rounder edges as you can cut in one long stroke rather than short, choppy strokes. Finally, determine if you prefer straight handles or scissor-style handles. I prefer scissor-style handles, but some people (especially those who are left-handed), prefer the palm grip of a straight-handled shear. If you do choose a straight-handle shear, I highly recommend making sure the shears have a spring. It makes cutting much faster and is easier on your hands.

TEXTURED EARRING TRIO

These simple earring designs will give you an opportunity to practice the technique of texturing wire with brass texture plates and a pasta machine.

Tools
- stepped roundnose pliers
- chainnose pliers
- metal hole-punch pliers (1.25 mm)
- metal hole screw punch
- wire cutters
- metal shears
- pasta machine with brass texture plates of your choice
- small metal files, such as diamond files (or an emery board)

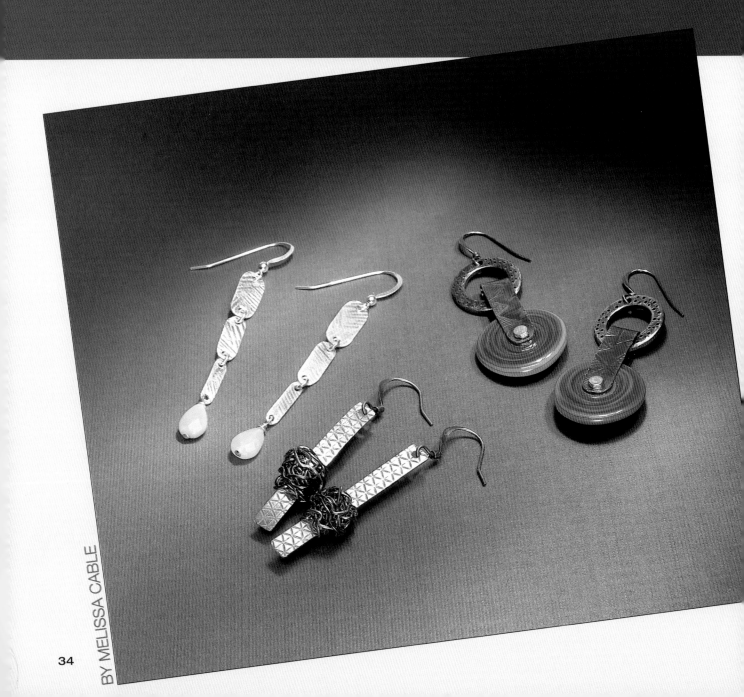

BY MELISSA CABLE

Pacific Northwest Rain

Texture the strip wire (p. 32–33). Cut each piece in half and round the corners as desired using your shears and/or metal files. Punch a hole on each end of the strip wire pieces with the 1.25 mm hole-punch pliers. Attach the strip wire together with jump rings, as shown, starting with the ¼-in. (6.5 mm) piece, the ³⁄₁₆-in. (5 mm) piece in the middle, and the ⅛-in. (3 mm) piece. Wire-wrap a bead to the bottom of each ⅛-in. strip wire piece. Attach an earring wire to the ¼-in. piece. Make a second earring.

Materials
- **2** 8 mm teardrop beads
- 1 in. (25.5 mm) ¼-in. (6.5 mm) 24-gauge strip wire
- 1 in. (25.5 mm) ³⁄₁₆-in. (5 mm) 24-gauge strip wire
- 1 in. (25.5 mm) ⅛-in. (3 mm) 24-gauge strip wire
- **6** 2½ mm ID, 20-gauge jump rings
- **2** 1 in. (25.5 mm) headpins
- pair of earring wires

Textured Tumbleweeds

Materials
- 3 in. (76 mm) ³⁄₁₆-in. (5 mm) 24-gauge strip wire
- 4 ft. (1.22 m) 24-gauge wire, dead-soft
- pair of earring wires

Cut the strip wire in half. Texture the strip wire (p. 32–33). File the edges smooth. With the 1.25 mm hole-punch pliers, punch a hole at the top of each strip. Punch another hole ½ in. (13 mm) from the bottom and string a 2 ft. (61.0 cm) piece of 24-gauge wire halfway through. Loosely and randomly wrap each end in opposite directions, creating a coiled bead around the strip wire. When you begin to run out of wire, twist the two ends together on the backside, trim, and tuck the ends inside the coil. Use roundnose pliers to gently twist kinks in the wire to both add interest and tighten the wires. Attach an earring wire to the top. Make a second earring, being sure to match the coil sizes.

Grandfather Clock

These earrings match the Grandfather Clock pendant that follows on p. 36. Materials are listed here. See the next page for full instructions.

Materials
- **2** 20 mm lampworked disks
- **2** brass bolts and nuts, no larger than 2.2 mm in diameter
- **2** 16 mm OD washers
- 4 in. (10.2 cm) ¼-in. (6.5 mm) 24-gauge strip wire
- pair of earring wires

GRANDFATHER CLOCK

Members of two generations of Cable family have grandfather clocks in their living rooms. Whenever I visit, I am mesmerized by the rhythmic movement of the pendulum. The gentle sway of this pendant as I wear it reminds me of these special clocks.

Materials
- 30 mm lampworked disk
- brass bolt and nut, no larger than 2.2 mm in diameter
- 18 OD mm washers
- 2½ in. (64 mm) ¼ in. (6.5 mm) 24-gauge strip wire

Tools
- stepped roundnose pliers
- heavy-duty wire cutters
- metal hole screw punch
- metal shears
- household hammer
- chasing hammer
- steel bench block
- center punch or other metal stamp
- pasta machine
- brass texture plates
- small metal files, such as diamond files (or an emery board)

Recommended Cord:
KD, CH

BY MELISSA CABLE

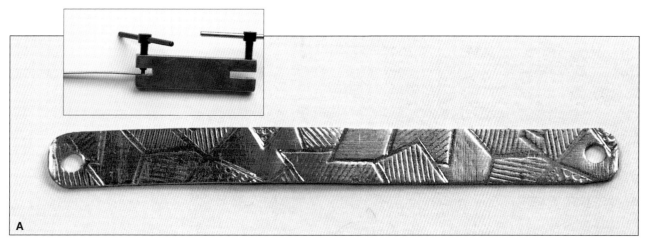

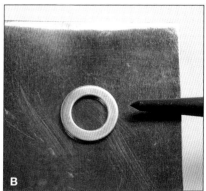

A Cut the strip wire in half (for earrings only). Texture the strip wire (p. 32–33). Punch a hole in the center of each end of the strip wire using the 2.3 mm (largest) peg on a screw punch.

B Texture the washer with a center punch or other stamp.

C Using stepped roundnose pliers, bend the strip wire in half so the two end-holes align. Slide the washer onto the bent strip wire. Slide the lampworked disk between the holes and thread a bolt through all three holes. Secure the bolt with a nut.

D Trim the bolt with heavy-duty wire cutters and lightly tap the cut end with the rounded side of a chasing hammer to rivet it into place, preventing the nut from coming off (a tip shared by artist Robert Dancik).

For earrings only: Punch a hole in each washer using the smaller peg on the screw punch and attach a earring wires.

GARDEN GATE

Strip wire is the perfect thickness to weave. It holds its shape, but is flexible enough to manipulate. The trick to making this pendant nice and square is to run wire through the spacers at the very end, so try to select spacers that have larger holes.

Materials
- **48** 5 mm daisy spacers
- **12–16** 3 mm beads
- flower or other charm
- jump ring or bail
- 1½ ft. (45.7 cm) ⅛-in. (3 mm) 24-gauge sterling silver strip wire
- 2 ft. (61.0 cm) 26-gauge sterling silver wire
- 1 ft. (30.5 cm) 24-gauge or 22-gauge sterling silver wire
- 1 ft. (30.5 cm) flexible beading wire, .010
- 6 in. 18-gauge craft wire
- 6 in. 22-gauge craft wire

Tools
- roundnose pliers
- chainnose pliers
- wire cutters
- pasta maker
- brass texture plates

Recommended Cord: SK, SD

BY MELISSA CABLE

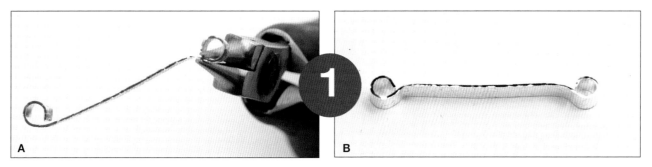

Step 1: Texture the wire

Cut eight 2-in. (51 mm) pieces of strip wire. Texture the pieces (p. 32–33).

A Make a loop at each end of each wire.

B Center the loops by placing roundnose pliers into the completed loop and pulling forward. Make sure all the pieces are the same length.

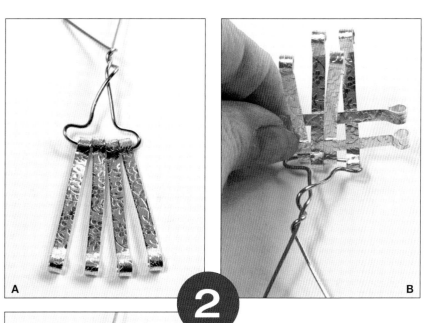

Step 2: Weave the wire

A String four wires onto a piece of 22-gauge craft wire and loop them together so there is just a little wiggle room. These are the stakes. The remaining four pieces of wire are the weavers.

B The easiest way to weave is to start at the open end of the stakes and then slide the weavers down. It will look messy at first. Don't worry! Weave one weaver under, over, under, and over the stakes and push toward the craft wire as far as it can go. Repeat with another weaver, this time going over, under, over, and under, pushing as far as it will go. Weave the third weaver under, over, under, and over.

C Weave the fourth weaver over, under, over, and under. This one can be hard and may require you to bend the stakes a bit. Once it's in, however, the loops on the bottom of the stakes should hold it in. The piece will likely look messy at this point; do not be concerned. The weave will straighten itself out in the next step.

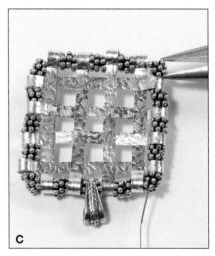

3

Step 3: Add the spacers

A Cut 1 ft. (30.5 cm) of beading wire. String three spacers and go through a strip wire loop. Repeat. Continue around the pendant. On one side in the center, string a bail in place of the middle spacer. Leave the craft wire on until you have one or two sides strung with spacers, but be sure to cut it off after that.

B Once you reach the other end, tie the two ends together (it's best to tie at the front of the first set of spacers so the knot can hide under the first wire). Don't worry if the corners look messy. We'll fix them next!

C Cut four pieces of 22- or 24-gauge wire (depending on what will go through the spacer holes). Make sure your spacers are lined up to match the spacers on the opposite side of the gate. Run each wire through all the spacers on one side.

D On the ends where the wire extends from the spacers, make a small coil and tuck it down flat onto the end spacer.

E, F On the ends where the wire extends from the strip wire loop, tuck the wire back behind the loop.

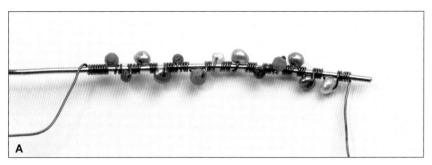

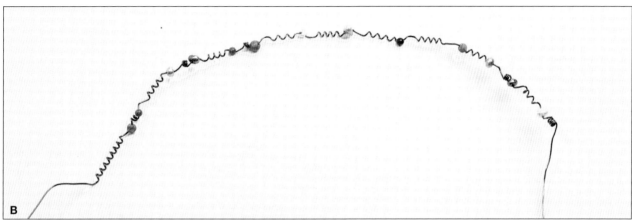

Step 4: Create the bead embellishment

A Leaving a 2-in. (51 mm) tail, coil the 26-gauge sterling silver wire around 18-gauge craft wire, adding a bead every 2–4 coils until you have 8–16 beads on (or as many as desired).

B Remove the coil from the craft wire and gently pull it apart until you have a longer piece of wire that is curly and has beads dotted along it.

C Use the 2-in. tail to secure a charm to the front of the gate and then weave the rest of the wire and beads onto the face of the gate as desired, being sure not to pull too hard or you will lose your curly coil (although, I do prefer to pull the coils flat when they end up on the backside of the pendant).

BRICK PATH

BL **PT**

This project is all about texture! Just as beautiful with one texture as it is with 10, this bracelet is a great way to showcase the patterns that brass texture plates have to offer. You'll create strip bricks and weave them together in a right-angle weave pattern, forming a textured path that is suitable for women or men.

Materials
- **2** large-hole accent beads
- 4 ft. (1.22 m) ⅛-in. (3 mm) wide 24-gauge strip wire
- 2 ft. (61.0 cm) 24-gauge craft wire
- 3¼ ft. (83.8 cm) 2 mm Ultrasuede
- hook or 15 mm large lobster claw clasp

Tools
- roundnose pliers (stepped preferred)
- chainnose pliers
- metal shears
- pasta maker
- brass texture plates
- awl
- 1-in. (25.5 mm) wide painter's tape

BY MELISSA CABLE

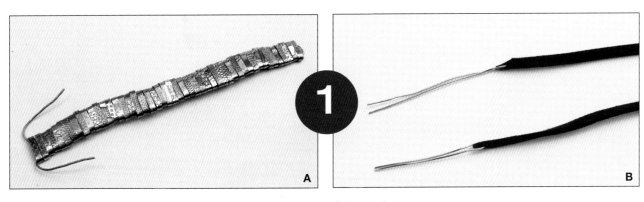

Hints

You don't have to string four vertical bricks. You can string three or five to get a different look. You can also make the bracelet wider. Just be sure that the height of the stacked horizontal brick panel is just under the height of one vertical brick. Keep in mind, however, that you will need more or fewer bricks depending on your design.

Step 1: Create the bricks

Cut 42 1-in. (25.5 mm) pieces of ⅛-in. (3 mm) wide 24-gauge strip wire.

Texture the pieces (p. 32–33).

Using the second step on a pair of stepped roundnose pliers, roll a loop on each end of the strip wire. Make sure the loops are closed and the textured side of the strip wire is flat and not bowed. The finished bricks should be about 13 mm long.

A Fold a 2-ft. piece of 24-gauge craft wire in half. String all the bricks (one loop through each strip wire loop). Add patina and polish the bricks (p. 106). Remove the craft wire.

B Test the hole sizes as you go by first cutting a 3-in. (76 mm) piece of Ultrasuede and folding it in half. Use an awl to pierce each end of the Ultrasuede. String a 4-in. (10.2 cm) piece of 24-gauge craft wire through each hole, bending it in half to form a needle. Test to see that you can string both needles through the bricks. The Ultrasuede should be snug. Remove the Ultrasuede and set it aside so you can test random links along the way to make sure you are rolling consistent size holes.

Step 2: Weave the pieces together

Use a simple two-needle right-angle weave to stitch the bricks together, as described below.

A Lay out your bricks as they will appear on your bracelet so you can make sure you have like sizes together and have mixed the textures evenly across the bracelet.

Cut a 3-ft. (91.4 cm) piece of Ultrasuede. Trim the ends of the Ultrasuede to a point and use an awl to pierce a hole in each end of the Ultrasuede. Place a craft wire needle on each end as you did in Step 1B. You may need to re-trim and replace the needle a few times during the project. String and center the clasp on the Ultrasuede.

B String four bricks over both Ultrasuede ends.

C String three bricks on one side of the Ultrasuede, as shown.

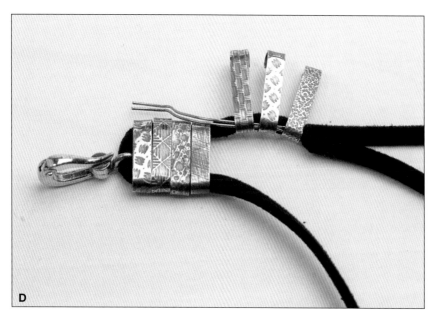

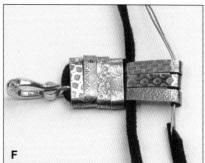

Step 2 continued

D String the other side of the Ultrasuede through the same brick loops as Step 2C, but string the Ultrasuede in from the opposite direction. This is best achieved one brick at a time.

E When the Ultrasuede is through all three loops, pull everything tight and into position. You will have four vertical bricks and three horizontal bricks.

F String one Ultrasuede end through the open horizontal brick loops.

G String the other Ultrasuede end through the same loops, but from the opposite side. Spread out the links or string the Ultrasuede through one loop at a time if needed.

H When the Ultrasuede is through all three loops, pull everything tight and into position. Make sure the Ultrasuede along the side is laying nicely and isn't twisted.

I Repeat Steps 2C–H until you reach the desired length. Be sure to pull tightly each time. It is extremely difficult to go back and adjust the tension later on. The Ultrasuede will stretch slightly, so it's better to have it too tight than too loose.

J Try to always end with horizontal links so the links do not slide into the clasp area. When you are done, simply tie an overhand knot into the remaining Ultrasuede. Embellish the ends as desired and trim.

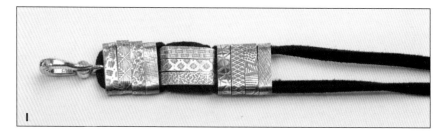

CONTINUUM CUFF

While strip wire provides a perfect canvas to showcase texture, it does not have the strength to become a stand-alone structure. Therefore, when you use long pieces of it, you always need to think about ways to support it. These could include using thicker gauge round wires, or connecting the strip together. This bracelet is a wonderful example of how to create structure with strip wire.

Materials (7.5-in./19 cm bracelet)
- **5** 10 mm lampworked beads
- **4** 8 mm metal beads (with holes big enough to fit 14-gauge wire)
- 22 in. (55.9 cm) ⅜-in. 24-gauge strip wire
- 8 in. 14-gauge wire
- 1 ft. (30.5 cm) 16-gauge wire
- 5 ft. 22-gauge wire

Tools
- stepped roundnose pliers
- chainnose pliers
- metal square-hole punch pliers
- wire cutters
- metal shears
- pasta machine
- brass texture plates
- painter's tape
- metal files, emery board, or sandpaper
- bracelet mandrel or can

BY MELISSA CABLE

Step 1: Create the textured strips

A Using the patchwork texturing method (p. 33), texture two 8-in. (20.3 cm) pieces of ⅜-in. (9.5 mm) strip wire. Texture the remaining 6 in. (15.2 cm) of strip wire in the same manner.

Using stepped roundnose pliers, roll the ends of the two 8-in. pieces so the final length of the strip wire is 7 in. (17.8 cm). Make sure the loops are large enough to accommodate a 14-gauge wire.

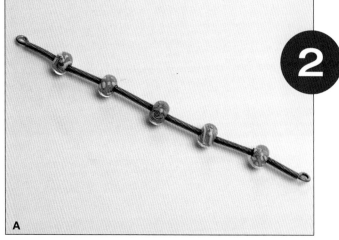

Step 2: Create the coiled bead section

Coil 4 ft. (1.22 m) of 22-gauge wire around a 14-gauge wire mandrel or an ¹⁄₁₆- (1.5 mm) in. dowel to create 6 in. of coiled wire.

A Cut the coil into 6 equal pieces. String an alternating pattern of coils and lampworked beads on 14-gauge wire. The total length of coiled wire and beads should be 7 in. Trim the two end coils as needed. Roll the ends of the 14-gauge wire into two equal loops large enough to fit a 14-gauge wire.

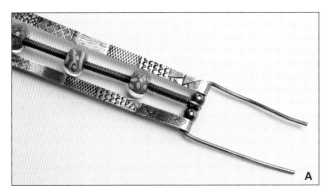

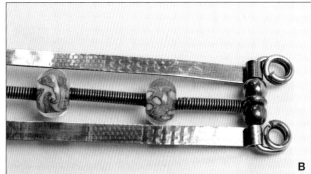

Step 3: Assemble the bracelet and construct a clasp

A On a 6-in. piece of 16-gauge wire, string a strip wire piece, an 8 mm bead, the coiled lampworked bead section, another 8 mm bead, and a strip wire piece. Bend the ends of the 16-gauge wire 90 degrees to hold everything in place. Repeat on the other side, making sure the strip wires and the coiled lampworked section are exactly the same length.

B On one side, roll each end of the 16-gauge wire into a double loop toward the back of the bracelet. Trim the ends.

C On the other side, fold the 16-gauge wires in half. Roll each folded 16-gauge wire into a hook toward the right side of the bracelet. Coil 22-gauge wire below the hook.

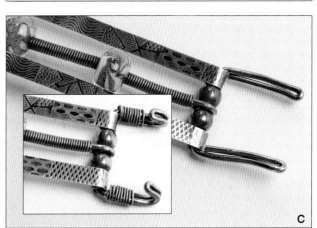

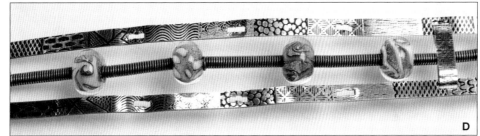

D On each strip wire, centered between each lampworked bead, use a square-hole punch to punch four adjacent square holes to create a slot. Make sure the slots line up with each other on each strip wire. Do not punch slots between the last lampworked beads and the end of the bracelet. Use a small file or thinly cut strip of sandpaper to file the slots smooth.

E Cut the remaining 6 in. of textured strip wire into 1½-in. (38 mm) pieces. On one piece, make a 90-degree bend ¼ in. (6.5 mm) from the end and thread it into one of the slots on the bracelet. Make a 90-degree bend on the other end and thread it into the corresponding slot on the opposite strip wire.

F Use chainnose pliers to fold the wire tightly closed. Repeat with the remaining 1½-in. strips and slots.

Carefully bend the bracelet into a circle on a bracelet mandrel, can, or other round item. The strip wires will want to bend at angles rather than smooth arcs, so do this slowly. Fit it to your wrist, pressing it into an oval, as desired. Adjust hooks to fit the double loops created in Step 3B.

DREAMING OF PUMPKINS

I'm fascinated with ways to cage and capture objects. I'm a collector of odds and ends, stones and glass, caps and shells. I am always trying to find a way to incorporate them into my jewelry so I can carry them with me. In this project, you'll learn to create a form to work around, allowing you to customize the shape of the pendant. This project combines some of the wire weaving skills you just practiced in Chapter 1 with the textured strip technique introduced in this chapter.

PT

Materials
- 18–22 mm found item such as a bead
- 3 ft. (91.4 cm) 16-gauge wire
- 2 ft. (61.0 cm) copper restrip
- 3–5 ft. 22-gauge wire
- **4–6** squares toilet tissue
- **2** tbsp. flour

Tools
- roundnose pliers
- chainnose pliers
- wire cutters
- pasta machine
- brass texture plates
- bowl

Recommended Cord: CH

BY MELISSA CABLE

Step 1: Create the form

If your found object can stand going into the oven at 250 degrees, as my glass heart did, you can roll it into the center of the form, reducing the amount of materials you have to remove from the center of your cage later. Otherwise, add your found object into the cage at the start of Step 3.

A Create a runny paste using 2 tbsp. of flour and 4 tbsp. of water in a small bowl. Roll your found object in two squares of toilet tissue and quickly dip into the paste. Roll the tissue into a ball, squeezing tightly as you go, removing the excess paste. Add more tissue, one square at a time, dipping it in the paste and squeezing it out each time until you have the size form you desire. The sample, as shown is approximately 1 in. (25.5 mm).

B Place the form on a cookie sheet in an oven at 250 degrees for at least 30 minutes, checking every 10 minutes to make sure it's not burning. Turn it over now and again to keep it from burning to the sheet and to prevent flat spots. It will be done when the form has hardened completely. If the found object inside is just glass (as shown in the sample), you can put it in your microwave for 30 second increments. In the microwave, my form took a total of 2½ minutes to harden.

Use a chasing hammer, if necessary, to slightly hammer away bulges or round out edges that surround flat spots. Do this carefully, as you do not want to crack the form.

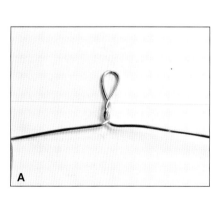
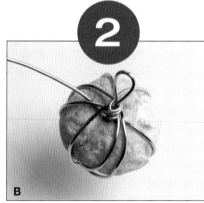

Step 2: Create the wire base

A Create a loop in the middle of a 3 ft. (91.4 cm) piece of 16-gauge wire. I use an elongated loop to mimic a pumpkin stem.

B Hold the "stem" against the form and wrap the wires around the form, wrapping them around the stem with each pass.

C Continue wrapping until you have approximately 4 in. (10.2 cm) of wire left. Wrap once around the stem and do not trim. Use chainnose pliers to kink the wires (p. 23), tightening them and providing an interesting embellishment.

Step 3: Add the textured strip

Texture 2 ft. (61.0 cm) of copper restrip wire using the patchwork method (p. 33), if desired. Cut into three equal pieces. Add patina and polish if desired.

A Attach one piece of the restrip by looping it around one of the base wires near the stem f the pumpkin. Wrap the strip around the form and loop it to a base wire on the opposite side of the stem.

Repeat this twice more until you have six ribs evenly spaced around the pumpkin.

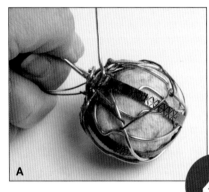
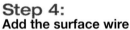

Step 4:
Add the surface wire

Add patina to the 22-gauge wire if desired and string it under a base wire until it's halfway through. Attach it to the base wire by wrapping it around the wire once.

A Begin to weave the 22-gauge wire around the pumpkin, going under and around the base wires, which will both help secure everything together and provide another layer of texture. After you finish weaving one end of the wire, weave the remaining end of the wire, covering all open spaces as needed.

Add more wire at any time to achieve the look you desire. When you are finished weaving the wire, use chainnose pliers to gently kink each wire a quarter turn to tighten.

B, C Coil 2 ft. (61.0 cm) of 22-gauge wire around the 16-gauge tail from Step 2C, rolling the end of the tail to keep the coil in place. Wrap the coiled tail around a dowel to create a curly coil. Shape as desired.

Step 5: Dissolve the form

Place the pumpkin in a bowl of hot water and let it sit for a moment. Using a pair of pliers, begin to poke and pull at the form, pulling out pieces as you go. The last little pieces can be rinsed out by holding the entire pumpkin under running water.

Chapter 3 • Corrugated Wire

Simple corrugation makes gentle ripples in the metal, creating places to tuck beads or to provide a surface embellishment that does not overpower the design. It's a texturing technique, but the texture is subdued.

SPOTLIGHT
Tips and Techniques

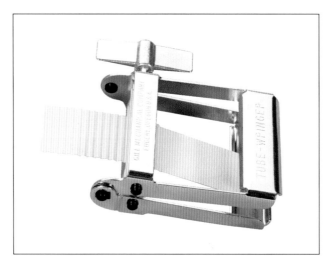

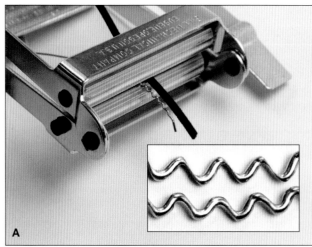

General corrugating tips

Traditionally metal corrugation in the jewelry world is done using a several-hundred-dollar table-mounted corrugator. However, over the years, artists have discovered that simple corrugation can be achieved with a tool originally used to squeeze out industrial gels and pastes from tubes. This tool, known as a tube wringer, relies on pressure from your hand to regulate the depth of the ripples, so how strong you are and how thick your metal is will greatly affect the overall corrugation process. Here are some guidelines to get you started:

• For strip wire, I find that the wider the piece of wire, the thinner the gauge of metal I choose. For example, while I can easily corrugate a piece of 24-gauge, ¼-in. (6.5 mm) wide sterling silver strip wire, a 24-gauge piece that is 1 in. (25.5 mm) wide is considerably harder for me to achieve deep consistent ripples.
• Round wire can be more difficult to corrugate than strip wire because too much pressure will cut the wire.
• Always start with dead-soft wire. The wire is going to get extremely hard by going through the corrugation process, so if you start with hard wire, the wire will end up brittle and will likely break.
• I generally do not go thicker than 18 gauge when I corrugate round wire and 24 gauge when I corrugate strip wire. However, as mentioned, I will often adjust my gauges down if the wire I am corrugating is wide.
• The effectiveness of corrugating will vary for everyone, so it's best to practice using copper or brass.

How to corrugate round wire

Corrugating wire takes a practiced hand. Learning how much pressure to place on the tube wringer can be hit or miss when you first start. I recommend using a piece of 2 mm Ultrasuede in the tube wringer at the same time you are corrugating your wire. This will minimize the chance that you will accidentally squeeze too hard and cut the wire. You can reuse the piece of Ultrasuede three or four times before it becomes too compacted and needs replacing. Over time, you will end up with extra pieces of corrugated Ultrasuede, so I've included a fun earring project that uses these wavy fibers. Some people find that they prefer to hold the corrugator in their stronger hand and turn with their weaker hand. Others prefer the opposite. You will determine your own preference after a few practice runs.

A Place the wire and Ultrasuede ends in the corrugator from the inside. Always leave enough uncorrugated wire on both ends to roll any loops you may need to. The direction you turn the handle depends on how you are holding the tool. Turn the handle in such a way that the wire moves away from your hand.

Practice counting the clicks and noticing the resulting number of ripples. Look at the shape of the ripples. Are they deep enough? Are they too shallow? Adjust your pressure as needed to create the ripples you desire. However, it's important to note that you can create ripples that are too deep. If your ripples are too deep, you will notice that the wire on one wall of the ripple will be thinner (inset). This means that the wire was slightly crushed, and a brittle, fragile place was created in your wire. It is likely the wire will break at this point. Allow it to break and set the good part of the wire aside to use in one of the earring projects featured in this chapter.

How to corrugate strip wire

While you are unlikely to break strip wire while corrugating it, you do run the risk of deforming it or creating uneven ripples. When you run long pieces of strip wire through the corrugator, it can tend to arc sideways, just as the wire did in the poor-man's rolling mill featured in Chapter 2. This is a result of uneven side-to-side pressure. Uneven ripples with varying depths are caused by inconsistent downward pressure. Both of these problems are inevitable as your hand gets tired and the pressure changes. To minimize these problems, work in small sections using these tricks I learned in a class with Jack Berry who, literally, wrote the book on microfolding:

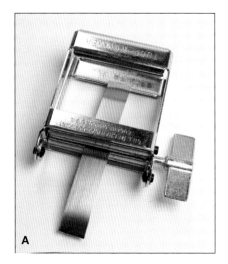
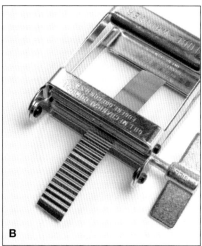

A Place the strip wire into the tube wringer in the middle of the wire length, rather than the end. Squeeze tightly and corrugate one end.

B Flip the piece around and place it back into the tube wringer, resting the first groove you made onto the roller until it's seated. Corrugate the second end of the strip wire.

SPOTLIGHT Tools

Tube wringer

Here are a few other considerations for working with a tube wringer. When you corrugate metal, especially wire, the metal will slightly eat into the rollers on the tube wringer. This is normal and not preventable. The downside of this is that these grooves will mar the surface of your wire, which is especially noticeable on wider strip wires. So be prepared to lightly sand your pieces after you corrugate them if you want a spotless appearance. You can also consider covering the strip wire with painter's tape before corrugating it. While it can be difficult to peel off tape that's been pressed down on the wire's surface, it does help minimize marring.

I have made it a habit to have one tube wringer that I use for wire and one that I use for sheet. You can also try to allocate a space on your tube wringer where you corrugate wire, and a space where you corrugate strip wire. Neither side will be groove free, but the strip wire side will have noticeably fewer scratches than the wire side.

Bail-making pliers

One of my favorite designs, the Rippled Bangle, was originally achieved using a metal dowel mounted in a vise. However, once these bail-making pliers became available, this project became incredibly easier and faster to complete. Bail-making pliers have two different size barrels that are uniform. This allows you to make perfect arches in two slightly different sizes. The beauty of this is that in creating a bracelet, we want the form to curve to fit our wrist. By having smaller arches on the inside of the bracelet, and larger arches on the outside, the bracelet will naturally form itself.

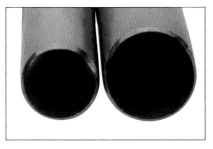

CORRUGATED EARRING COLLECTION

WW BL JR FP EW

Tools
• roundnose pliers
• chainnose pliers
• 1.25 mm hole-punch pliers
• wire cutters
• tube wringer
• chasing hammer
• steel bench block
• butane torch
• cross-locking tweezers
• 2 mm strip of Ultrasuede

When you first practice corrugating wire, you will undoubtedly break a few pieces. Although the instructions for these earrings call for making corrugated pieces, the earrings are designed to use up those broken bits of wire. There is also a pair of earrings that use the kinky Ultrasuede pieces you will begin to collect as you practice corrugating wire.

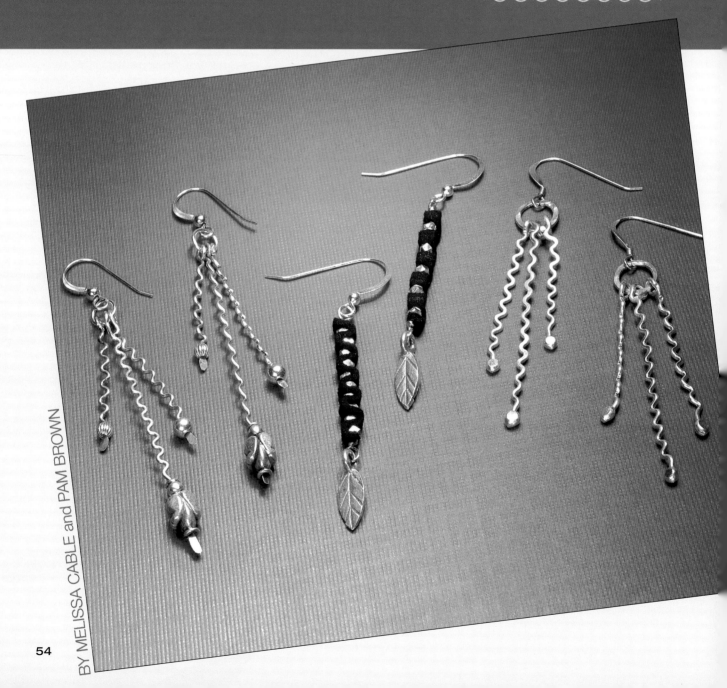

BY MELISSA CABLE and PAM BROWN

54

Materials
- **2** 6 mm ID, 18-gauge jump rings
- 1 ft. (30.5 cm) 18-gauge fine silver wire
- pair of earring wires

Pistols and Stamens

Cut the wire into two 2½-, two 2-, and two 3½-in. (64, 51, and 38 mm) lengths. Ball one end of each wire (p. 103). Place the wire in the corrugator so the ball is just extending from the rollers. Corrugate the wire, leaving ¼ in. (6.5 mm) of straight wire. If desired, lightly hammer the wires and jump rings flat. On each wire, roll a loop with the straight end. String one wire of each size on a jump ring and hang from an earring wire. Make a second earring.

Materials
- **6** beads that will fit on 18-gauge wire
- **2** 5 mm ID, 18-gauge jump rings
- 1 ft. (30.5 cm) 18-gauge wire, dead soft
- pair of earring wires

Bead Embellished Stamens

Cut the wire into two 2½-, two 2-, and two 1½-in. (64, 51, and 38 mm) lengths. Make a hammered headpin with each wire by hammering one end flat using a chasing hammer and bench block. String the beads onto the wires. Place a beaded wire into the corrugator so the bead is extending just beyond the rollers. Corrugate the wire, leaving ¼ in. (6.5 mm) of straight wire. Repeat with all the beaded wires. On each wire, roll a loop with the straight end using roundnose pliers. String one wire of each size on a jump ring and hang from an earring wire. Make a second earring.

Swinging Suede

Pick one side of the Ultrasuede to be the front. Using the 1.25 mm hole-punch pliers, punch 11 holes in the recessed areas of the corrugated Ultrasuede. If the holes do not punch cleanly, use wire cutters to snip off any Ultrasuede hanging from the holes. Trim the Ultrasuede in the recessed areas that proceed the first hole and follow the last hole. Cut the 24-gauge wire in half and wire-wrap a charm to one end. String the wire into the first hole on a piece of Ultrasuede. Add a bead on the wire. Carefully string the wire into the second hole. Add a bead. Repeat until the wire comes through the 11th hole. Make a wrapped loop and attach to an earring wire. Make a second earring.

Materials
- **20** 3 mm beads
- **2** charms
- **2** pieces 2-in. (51 mm) corrugated Ultrasuede (scrap)
- 3 in. (76 mm) 24-gauge wire
- pair of earring wires

BERRY VINES

BL WW PT

Materials
- coin, briolette, or other focal bead wire wrapped on a headpin if needed
- **100** 3 mm round beads
- **7** 4 mm ID jump rings
- 3 ft. (91.4 cm) 18-gauge wire, dead soft
- 20 ft. 28-gauge wire, dead soft
- clasp

Tools
- roundnose pliers
- chainnose or flatnose pliers
- wire cutters
- tube wringer corrugator
- ruler
- 9 in. (22.9 cm) 3 mm Ultrasuede cut into three 3-in. (76 mm) pieces

This necklace can be simple and understated or made into a fabulous statement piece, depending on what type of pendant you choose to frame. It works well with a variety of beads, from 3 mm round beads to seed-bead drops. You can also modify the design to wrap beads on both sides of the corrugated component.

BY MELISSA CABLE

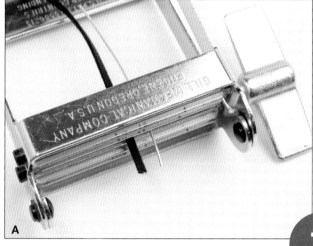

Step 1: Prepare the corrugated wire segments

A Place a piece of Ultrasuede and 3 in. (76 mm) of 18-gauge wire in the corrugator so ½ in. (13 mm) is extending from the rollers.

Corrugate the wire, counting 20 clicks. This will result in approximately 10 ripples, which we will refer to as peaks and valleys from this point forward. You want 10 peaks and 11 valleys.

B Look at the ripples and make sure the first and last ripple end at the top of a peak. Use chainnose pliers to flatten one end to make the end ripples match or to remove any excess ripples.

C Trim the wire so there is ½ in. of straight wire remaining on each side. Roll a loop on each end perpendicular to the ripples. Make eight segments.

1

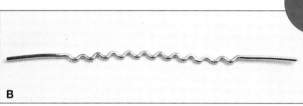

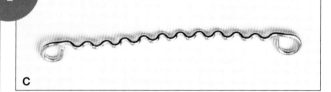

2

Step 2: Wrap wire, add beads, and connect

Hold a component so the peaks and valleys face you and the loops are to the back of the piece, as shown. This is the front of the component.

A Cut 24 in. (61 cm) of 28-gauge wire and string ¼ in. (6.5 mm) through the left-hand loop to anchor it. Using the longer side, wrap the wire around the peaks and valleys toward you, keeping the coil as tight as possible.

B Once you reach the other end, turn the piece over so you are looking at the back. The wire will be on the left again. Wrap two times AWAY from you until you reach the center of the first valley. String a bead on the wire and wrap the wire around the next valley, nestling the bead under the first peak. Repeat until 10 beads are strung. You may notice that less wire shows on the front, making the front look neat and tidy.

C When you are finished with the last bead, wrap twice and trim all tails and snug down the ends to make sure there are no sharp ends. Straighten the beads if needed and slightly arc the component.

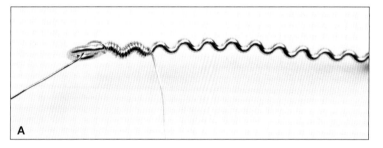

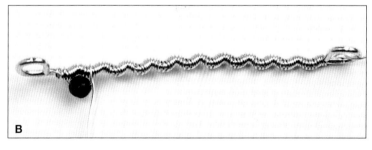

A

Step 3: Create the pendant frame and assemble

A Measure the perimeter of the pendant. Cut 18-gauge wire to twice this length plus 1 in. (25.5 mm). Corrugate the wire, leaving ½ in. (13 mm) on each end; roll a loop on each flat end. Wrap the peaks and valleys with wire and beads in the same manner as described in Step 2. Shape the component to frame the pendant. String a jump ring through one loop of the pendant frame, through the pendant, and then through the second loop of the pendant frame. Before closing the jump ring, string a component on each side. Close the jump ring. Continue assembling the necklace with jump rings. Attach a clasp half to each end.

EARRINGS

These earrings are made with the same components as the berry vines. The beads used are seed bead drops. Simply create a berry vine, shape it around a dowel, connect the two looped ends together with a 3.5 mm ID, 18-gauge jump ring, and hang from an earring wire.

ROUNDABOUT ROAD

This bracelet reminds me of trips through Europe over bumpy roads leading to massive roundabouts that were seemingly impossible to navigate. This bracelet is bound to become my driving talisman for all future European road trips ... complete with a lucky horseshoe on the end.

Materials
- 7½ in. (19.1 cm) 24-gauge ½-in. (13 mm) copper strip wire
- **4** 24 mm copper washers

Tools
- heavy-duty roundnose pliers
- chainnose pliers
- bail-making pliers
- heavy-duty wire cutters
- metal shears
- chasing hammer
- steel bench block
- tube wringer corrugator
- metal files
- marker

BY MELISSA CABLE

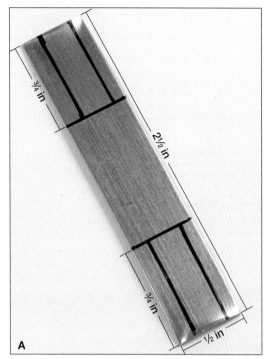

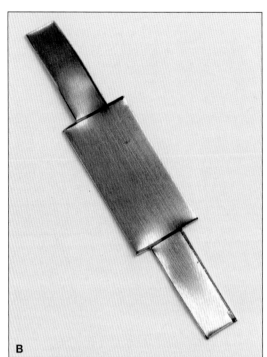

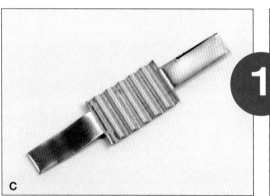

1

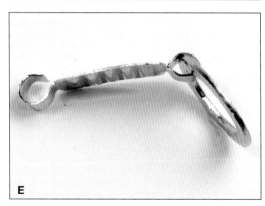

Step 1: Create the corrugated links

A Cut a 2½-in. (64 mm) piece of ½ in. (13 mm) copper strip wire. Make a mark ¾ in. (19 mm) from each end. Divide the section between the marks and the end of the wire into three sections measuring ⅛, ¼, and ⅛ in. (3, 6.5, and 3 mm).

B Using metal shears, cut off the two outer sections on each end, leaving a tab on each end.

C Place the strip wire in the corrugator and corrugate the wide middle section. Repeat Steps 1A and 1B twice for a total of three corrugated pieces.

D Hammer the edges and the tabs of the corrugated strip wire, flattening the ripples along the edges. Switch edges as you hammer, rather than going around the wire, otherwise, the piece will get distorted as it stretches out as a result of flattening the ripples. Create the same hammered texture on three washers.

E Use the smallest barrel on bail-making pliers to roll one tab into a loop, adjusting the loop back so it's centered on the strip wire. Repeat on the other end. Repeat with the remaining pieces. Gently arc the corrugated components so the bracelet forms to your wrist.

Connect the components together, starting with a washer. Use chainnose pliers to gently open and close the tab loops.

A

B

Step 2: Create the clasp

A Hammer one half of a washer. (Avoid work-hardening the part that will need to bend.)

B Using heavy-duty wire cutters, make a cut through the washer in the center of the unhammered area. Use roundnose pliers to roll each end back into hooks. When they are halfway rolled, you can use the rounded end of your chasing hammer to finish bending down the hooks and also create a hammered finish on them.

C File the edges of the hooks as needed. Place the washer on its side on a steel bench block and gently hammer until it's shaped like a horseshoe. You may need to place it flat on the steel bench block now and again to hammer it flat with a rawhide hammer. Attach to the last corrugated component and adjust the hooks as needed to fit into the washer on the other end.

Add patina and polish as desired.

C

TIP: Annealing

Depending on the type and thickness of copper washer you use, you may find the clasp easier to form if you anneal the metal first. Annealing is the process of heating metal to a certain point that allows it to return to its original state. The metal becomes dramatically softer, and therefore, easier to manipulate. To accomplish this, heat the washer with a butane torch on a fireproof surface, such as a firebrick or soldering pad, until it glows orange. This may be easier to see by working in a dark or dimly lit room. Quench the washer in water to cool it. You will notice the washer turns black with oxidation. Some of the oxidation will have been removed by quenching. You will need to use a scouring pad or steel wool to scrub off the rest of it—although soaking in ketchup also works (the acid in ketchup acts similar to pickling acids used by jewelers).

RIPPLED BANGLE

While you can use a textured wire for this project, such as one created using the poor-man's rolling mill method (Chapter 2), or by creating a hammered finish (p. 104), the harder the wire is, the harder it will be to make the ripples. You may want to consider sticking with a less-aggressive texture, such as the satin or stardust finish (p. 105).

Materials
- **15** 6 mm round beads
- **15** 4 mm round beads
- 15 in. ¼-in. (6.5 mm) wide 24-gauge strip wire
- 1 ft. (30.5 cm) .014 beading wire, color to match strip wire
- **2** 2 x 2 mm crimp beads
- **2** small crimp covers (optional)
- magnetic clasp

Tools
- roundnose pliers
- bail-making pliers
- chainnose pliers
- crimping pliers
- 1.8 mm hole-punch pliers or the smaller peg on a screw-type two-hole punch
- metal shears
- ruler
- marker

BY MELISSA CABLE

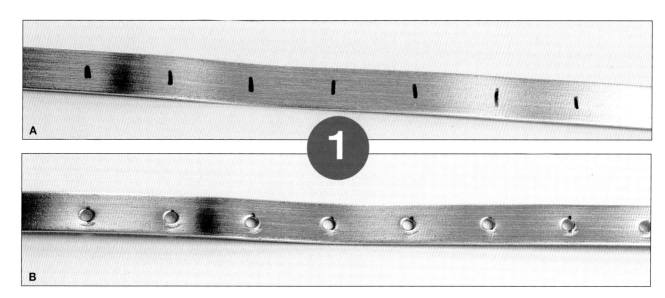

Step 1: Prepare the wire

A Starting 24 mm from one end, make a centered mark every 12 mm. (It is important to stick with the metric measurements here for accuracy.)

B Using hole-punch pliers or a screw punch, punch holes on each of the marks until you have the number of holes required to achieve your desired length: 26 holes for 6½ in. (16.5 cm), 28 holes for 7 in. (17.8 cm) or 30 holes for 7½ in. (19.1 cm). If you need to decrease or increase the size, always do it in increments of two holes and make sure you always have at least 12 mm of unpunched wire on each end. If using plain wire, use sandpapers to remove any light scratches (p. 108). Patina and polish, if desired.

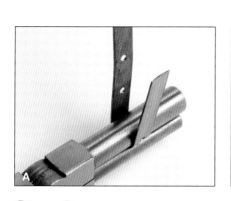
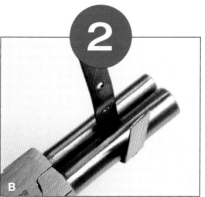
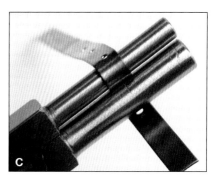
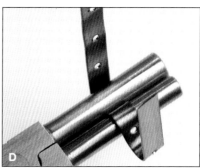

Step 2: Create the ripples

A Hold the bail-making pliers perpendicular to the table with the large barrel directly between the first two holes, and bend both sides of the wire up evenly.

B Without removing the pliers from the bend, open the pliers and rotate them so they are now parallel to the table.

C Bend the wire down over the small barrel.

D Without removing the pliers from the bend, open the pliers and rotate them 180 degrees, keeping them parallel to the table. Bend the wire up around the large barrel of the pliers.

Repeat Steps 2B–2D until you have ripples between all of your holes. The holes will better align themselves as the bracelet gets shaped in Step 3. The top of the bracelet will be the side that has both ends facing up, has large wells, and has small ripples.

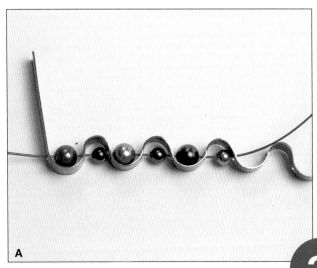

Step 3: Add the beads and clasp

By placing larger beads on the top (outside) of the bracelet, and smaller beads on the bottom (inside) of the bracelet, the bracelet will somewhat self-shape itself.

A Cut a 1 ft. (30.5 cm) piece of beading wire. String the first hole and a 6 mm bead. String the next hole and a 4 mm bead. Repeat until all beads are strung. The 6 mms will be on the top and the 4 mms on the bottom. If the bracelet curves over itself during these steps, skip back and forth between squeezing large and small wells to help refine the shape.

Use your fingers to squeeze all of the smaller wells (the ones that hold the 4 mm beads) together. The bracelet will curve dramatically.

Now, squeeze all of the larger wells together, which will slightly uncurve the bracelet, leaving a more gentle arc.

B Shape the bracelet as desired. Attach a magnetic clasp half to each wire end using crimp beads.

C Cut the ends of the strip wire to ½ in. (13 mm) above the hole. Roll the wire into a half circle with roundnose pliers, toward the clasp. Use chainnose pliers to close the circle into a tight loop.

D Gently roll the ends downwards, toward the clasp so their arc lines up with the arc of the ripples. Cover the crimp beads with crimp covers, if desired.

Chapter 4 • Heavy Wire

In previous chapters, we worked with heavier wires as a way to create frames and structure for fine-gauge woven wires. In this chapter, we'll explore using large-gauge wire as the star of the piece. Because of their size, 18-, 16- and 14-gauge wires not only create strong structures that stand alone, they provide a large enough surface area to showcase applied textures, such as a hammered finish. In most cases, because of the assertive presence of heavy-gauge wire, incorporated beads merely become accents—slight pops of color. But in our final project in this chapter, the Andromeda Cuff, the heavy wire showcases gorgeous handmade lampworked beads, an appropriate choice for the handcrafted look of heavy-gauge wire projects.

SPOTLIGHT
Tips and Techniques

How to minimize marring wire

Because this wire is more substantial, mars will be more noticeable. Marring heavier gauge wire is inevitable, because it often requires a firmer grip to work it into the desired shape. The secret to mar-free wire does not have as much to do with the wire as it does with the tools. Your tools should be as mar-free as possible, because scratches and dents in your tools will often "transfer" to the wire. Consider using a material such as Tool Magic to place a light rubber coat on your tools, allowing for better grip and less damage to the wire. It is easily removed or replaced, so it does not permanently alter your tools.

Also be sure to use the right pliers for the right job. For example, don't grip a wire with roundnose pliers, because they will leave a divot. Use chainnose or flatnose pliers to grip. And of course, while they provide good traction, serrated tools will wreak havoc on heavy-gauge wire!

Heavy-gauge spirals

Two of the projects featured in this section use spiral links created from heavy-gauge wires. Mastering the art of spiral making will allow you to create beautiful links, useful clasps, and fancy charms.

When starting any spiral, it's best to taper the wire end so the center circle can be as small as possible. This can be done by simply squeezing the wire several times with chainnose or flatnose pliers or by gently hammering the wire on a steel bench block with the flat side of a chasing hammer. Also, be sure the end of the wire does not extend past the edge of the pliers when forming the circle.

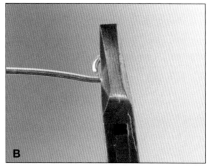

A Roll a small loop with the tapered end of the wire (If this loop will have a jump ring or other wire running through it at some point, be sure to size it accordingly.)

B Hold the flatnose pliers so they point to the ceiling. Hold the circle you just created so it's pointing up and just slightly sticking out from the pliers. The remaining wire will be parallel with the table.

C Push the wire up until it's pointing to the ceiling, rolling it around the center circle.

Readjust the entire piece back to the position as seen in Step B. Once again, push the wire up, pointing to the ceiling and using the previous circles as guides for the wire to follow. Repeat until the spiral is the desired size.

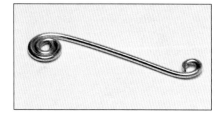

Two-sided spirals

If you are making a link that has a spiral on each side, be sure to start the spirals on opposite sides of the wire as shown, and alternate back and forth between each side as you roll the spiral so the spirals are even in size.

Open spirals

Open spirals are created in the same manner; however, rather than pushing the wire against the previous circles, simply use them as a guide to create a circle that is seated slightly away. When repositioning the spiral as in Step D above, use the pliers to hold the space between the spiral circles. Work in very small movements to help control the spacing and shape of the curves.

SPOTLIGHT Tools

Flatnose nylon jaw pliers

When working with wire of any gauge, the wire may become bent or arced in places that make shaping it inconvenient. Using chainnose or flatnose pliers to squeeze the wire straight again often creates new kinks and bends and mars the wire. Instead, consider using nylon jaw pliers. These pliers are generally a heavier version of traditional flatnose pliers with nylon caps covering the flat surface of the pliers. Simply grip the wire with these pliers and pull the pliers across the wire to straighten it. Like any metal, the more you work it, the harder it will become, so it's advisable to straighten wire only when absolutely needed.

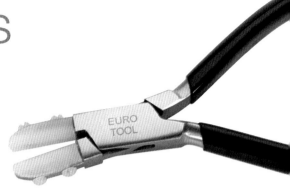

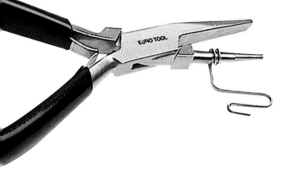

Stepped roundnose

Stepped roundnose pliers are a fantastic tool for bending consistent loops in wire. Generally, these pliers are constructed so one side of the pliers have a flat surface (often protected with a rubber cover to minimize marring), and the other barrel has a series of three round surfaces that increase in diameter with each step. The smallest roundnose pliers generally have steps that start at 2 mm; medium stepped pliers, also known as Wrap N Taps, have barrels that are 5 mm to 10 mm; and the largest pliers have steps that are 13 mm to 20 mm in diameter.

In addition to being a handy tool when dealing with heavy-gauge wire, stepped roundnose pliers are especially helpful when working with strip wire, as you did in Chapter 2. When you roll a loop at the end of strip wire using a pair of standard roundnose pliers, the roll is uneven and cone-like because it's following the shape of the graduated roundnose pliers. In order to get a consistent, even loop with standard roundnose pliers, you must switch the pliers back and forth between the two sides of the loop. With stepped roundnose pliers, you have a consistent diameter on which to bend your loop, allowing you to achieve a uniform loop every time.

SAM'S CHAIN

This chain was inspired by a necklace my 5-year-old nephew had in his box of goodies. His mom calls it his piece of bling. I was intrigued with it and had to draw out the basic design. After playing with wire for a bit, this is the version I came up with.

Here, we'll practice manipulating heavier wire with 18-gauge before graduating to 16- and 14-gauge wires later in the chapter.

Materials
- 6 ft. (1.8 m) 18-gauge fine or dead-soft sterling silver wire
- 4 mm ID 18-gauge jump ring
- clasp

Tools
- roundnose pliers
- chainnose pliers
- wire cutters
- 6 mm mandrel

BY PAM BROWN

Step 1: Pre-cut the wire
(Note: process photos show bracelet construction)

For a bracelet, cut the wire into 29 2¼-in. (57 mm) lengths. For a necklace, cut 18 5-in. (12.7 cm) lengths. You may want to cut a few less in case you don't need that many.

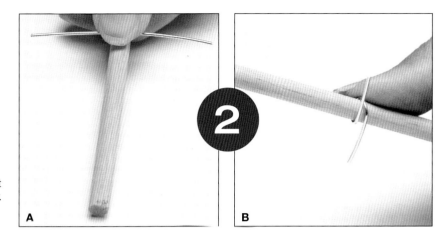

A

B

Step 2: Form the large circle

A For a bracelet, center a piece of the 2¼-in. wire over a 6 mm mandrel. For a necklace, use a 5-in. piece of wire and a 12 mm mandrel.

B Use your thumbs to wrap both sides of the wire around the mandrel to form a circle. Continue wrapping until the ends pass each other on the bottom of the mandrel. Remove the wire from the mandrel. Make sure your ends are equal.

Gently open the circle and string on one end of the clasp.

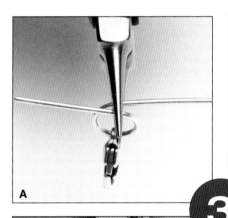

A

B

C

Step 3: Form the smaller circles

A Hold the link with roundnose pliers at the point where the two wire ends cross.

Pick a point on the pliers that you will use the whole time to make your circles. For a necklace, use the largest point of the pliers.

B Wrap the wire facing the back of the pliers until it points straight up, forming a smaller circle. Now you have formed one large and one small circle.

C Reposition the link in the pliers so the remaining wire faces the back of the pliers.

Repeat 3B. Both ends of the wire are now pointing up.

Step 3 continued:

D Insert pliers into all three rings, holding onto the small rings at their bottoms.

E Continue to wrap the wire that is facing the back of the pliers around the pliers to complete the circle.

F Remove the link from the pliers, flip it, and repeat. You will now have both end wires pointing out.

G Cut the wire ends at the top of the circles. Do this carefully because if you cut them too far back, you will feel the sharp ends once the chain is put together.

Make final adjustments by pushing the ends down (flush) and the circles together with a pair of chainnose pliers.

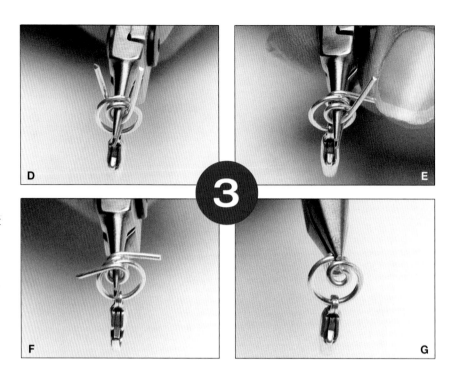

Step 4: Connect and finish

You made it through the first link. Now you are ready to start all over again for the next link. Make the second link as outlined in Steps 2 and 3, with one exception:

A After you form the first circle in Step 2, separate the wires at the top where they cross and string the link into the three circles on the previous link. This is critical!

Continue Steps 2–4 and connect the links until you reach the desired length. Use a jump ring to connect the other end of your clasp.

Run your hand down the length of chain to see if you feel any cut ends poking out. If you do, simply trim back the end. If it's cut too short already, use your pliers to roll it forward a bit, tightening the smaller circle.

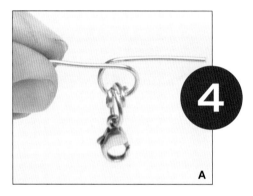

Hints
Be sure you connect each link as you go. Once a link is completely made, it cannot be connected to the previous one.

To make this bracelet as quickly as possible do it in assembly-line steps. For example, cut all of the wire, do all of the mandrel work in Steps 2 and 3, and then connect and finish each link. This makes for a much faster process.

To customize the size, consider that each inch of chain is made up of 4½ links and each link uses 2¼ in. of wire.

HEAVY METAL

Materials
- 15 mm x 10 mm briolette
- **4** 6 mm beads
- **8** 3 mm beads
- 5 ft. (1.5 m) 16-gauge wire
- 6½ ft. 24-gauge wire
- **4** 1½-in. (38 mm) headpins

Tools
- roundnose pliers
- chainnose pliers
- flatnose pliers
- wire cutters
- chasing hammer
- steel bench block

This project incorporates some of the weaving you practiced in Chapter 1. This project, made from a series of shimmering spirals woven together with fine gauge wire, features a pendant that is also a great stand-alone piece when simply attached to chain.

BY PAM BROWN

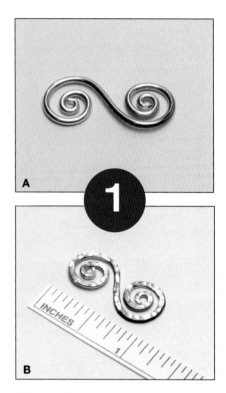

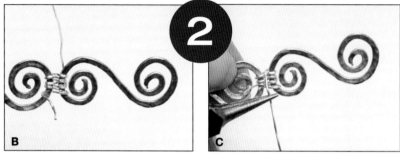

Step 1: Create the hammered open double spiral

Cut the 16-gauge wire into two 3½-in. (89 mm) lengths. The exact total needed will be dependent on your desired length and pendant design.

A Create a double-sided open spiral link (p. 66) with ¼ in. (6.5 mm) of wire between the spirals. The overall measurement of the link is 1 in. (25.5 mm)

Continue making spirals. Remember to make fewer links than you think you need initially, assemble the necklace, and then try it on before you make the last links. Differences in hammering, wrapping, and a number of things can make the chain different sizes, so yours may vary from mine.

Slightly flatten the spiral with the flat side of the chasing hammer and a steel bench block. If it begins to change shape, correct it as you go. Be sure half of the spirals lie in one direction and the other half lie in the opposite direction.

B Use the rounded end of the chasing hammer to create a hammered finish (p. 104).

Step 2: Connect the spirals

Cut a 4½-in. (11.4 cm) piece of 24-gauge wire if you are dangling beads. Otherwise, cut a 3½-in. piece.

A Place two matching spirals end-to-end, leaving approximately ⅛ in. (3 mm) between them. String the wire down and under the outermost circle on one spiral leaving a ½-in. (13 mm) tail so you have something to hold onto.

B Cross to the other spiral and go over and around the outermost circle. Cross the wire back over to the first spiral. Continue weaving figure 8s until there are a total of three weaves on the first spiral and four on the second spiral.

C, D Fold the wire straight down the face of the weaves. Grasp the wire just below the weaves and create a wrapped loop that is perpendicular to the spirals. Do not trim the tail.

TIP You can forego the wrapped loop if you do not want to dangle wire-wrapped beads between the spirals. Simply skip to Step 2E after folding the wire down the face of the weave.

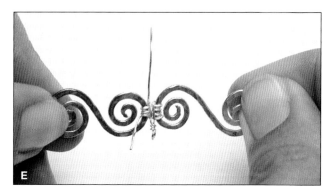

E Take the wrapped-loop tail and wrap it up the back of the weave, over, and down the face of the weave again, and finally up the back of the weave.

F Trim the initial tail and wrap the long tail around the first spiral to secure it, and create the fourth wrap so both sides are even. Bend the spirals back and forth to allow the weave to open up slightly and act as a hinge. Trim all tails. Repeat until both necklace sides are constructed. Each half has the spirals facing opposite directions.

String the beads on headpins and wire-wrap them to the loops extending from the weaves between the spirals.

Step 3: **Make the pendant**

Begin by taking two opposite-facing spirals from Step 1.

A For the top connector, cut a 2-in. (51 mm) piece of 16-gauge wire. Taper the ends and create small loops on each end, on the same side of the wire. Slightly start an open spiral on each side, just allowing the component to arch. (The unit measures about ¾ in./19 mm) Flatten and create a hammered finish (p. 104).

B Lay the pieces out as shown here or on p. 71. Use 3½ in. (89 mm) of 24-gauge wire to weave them together as you did in Step 2, but skip the wrapped loop and forgo the bending of the spirals to loosen the weave. If stringing onto chain, add chain before connecting the top connector to the spirals.

C Use another piece of 3½-in. wire to wrap the briolette to the center of the pendant, as shown.

Weave the pendant to each side of the necklace with 3½-in. of 24-gauge wire, connecting to the top connector formed in Step 3A.

BEJEWELED SPIRALS

This project uses closed spiral links that have centers large enough to fit a 16-gauge jump ring. Clustering beads onto these links creates a pop of color and texture, and makes for a fun way to customize this metal bracelet.

Materials
- **25** 3–4 mm beads or seed beads
- 3 ft. (91.4 cm) 16-gauge wire
- 8 ft. (2.4 m) 24-gauge wire

Tools
- roundnose pliers
- chainnose pliers
- flatnose pliers
- wire cutters
- **3–4** small skewers or dowels
- chasing hammer
- steel bench block

BY PAM BROWN

74

Step 1: Create the double spiral links

A Cut the 16-gauge wire into seven 2¾-in. (70 mm) segments. (More segments may be needed to reach desired length.)

Create seven closed double-sided spirals (p. 66), leaving ¼ in. (6.5 mm) between the two spirals and leaving a center hole large enough to fit a 16-gauge jump ring. The final length of the link will be approximately ¾–1 in. (19–25.5 mm).

> **Hint**
> When creating the spirals, flattening the end of the wire with pliers helps form a smoother circle.

Step 2: Hammer and embellish the spirals

A Slightly flatten the spiral with the flat side of the chasing hammer and a steel bench block. If it begins to change shape, correct it as you go. Be sure all spirals are lying in the same direction. Use the rounded end of the chasing hammer to create a hammered finish (p. 104).

B Cut a 6-in. piece of 24-gauge wire for each spiral. Use the first ½ in. (13 mm) of the wire as a handle and hold it with your nondominant hand. On a spiral link, begin wrapping the wire around the space between the two spirals to secure it.

C At this point you will be free-forming your work. Wrap your wire a bit around the link, add a bead, wrap, and so on until you are done with the wire and three beads are on. Don't try to be neat as you work; it's more interesting to let it look random.

D At any point you can go back and end the beginning wire by wrapping it around the initial link. Make sure that your cluster doesn't shift around on the spiral. If it does, make one wrap directly around the link and tighten to secure it from moving.

Trim if needed, and tuck the end of the wire into the wire cluster you just made using chainnose pliers.

Repeat for all the spirals.

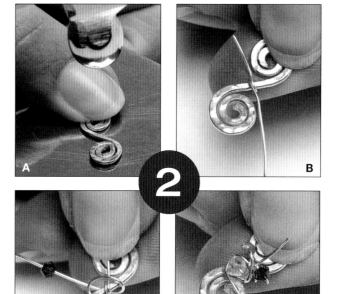

Step 3: Connect and embellish the links

Take 3–4 bamboo skewers and hold them together side by side. To help keep them flat, you may want to tape them together.

A Using 10 in. (25.4 cm) of 16-gauge wire, make a coil. Cut into jump rings (p. 101). Make the cuts across the top of the oval, not too close to the corners. These cuts will be covered in the next step.

Connect the spirals with the oval jump rings, keeping the cut edge on top.

B, C Using 4½ in. of 24-gauge wire, make a coil around the jump ring, hiding the cut. Start wrapping to the left of the cut heading toward the spiral, then push the coil down over the cut area and finish the coil. Trim as needed.

Step 4: Create and embellish an S-hook clasp

Create an S-clasp with 2½ in. (64 mm) of wire (p. 102). Hammer a finish on the clasp and embellish it with 1 ft. (30.5 cm) of 24-gauge wire as you did in Step 2, adding an extra bead or two.

CHARMING STORY

Materials
- beads, charms, chain pieces of your choice and with jump rings and headpins to attach
- 4 in. (10.2 cm) 14-gauge wire
- 1¼ in. (32 mm) 14-gauge fine silver wire

Tools
- ¾ in. (19 mm) wooden dowel
- chasing hammer
- steel bench block
- roundnose pliers
- chainnose pliers
- wire cutters
- butane torch
- cross-locking tweezers

Recommended Cord: KS, SK

To this day, I still have my charm necklace from childhood. My friend Brenda and I collected charms of all kinds … roller skates, our initials, and of course those best-friend charms you split in half. Now, living so far away from my dear friend, I was nostalgic for our fun times and created this updated version of a charm necklace while thinking of her. I call it Charming Story, because you can use the charms and beads you choose to construct a story for your piece.

BY MELISSA CABLE (designed by CORINNA VANKLEEK)

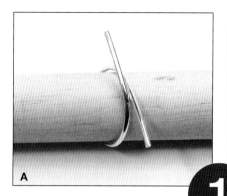

Step 1: Create the charm holder

A Wrap the 14-gauge wire around a ¾-in. (19 mm) wooden dowel until the wire crosses itself.

B Using chainnose pliers, make a 90-degree bend in the wire just before it crosses the other wire. Create a matching 90-degree bend on the other end of the wire.

C Using the flat side of a chasing hammer and steel bench block, flatten the charm holder to work-harden the piece. Use the rounded end of the hammer to make a hammered finish. Trim the straight wires to ½ in. (13 mm) long and roll them into loops.

Step 2: Create the charm holder bail bar and assemble

Wire-wrap beads into charms, making sure the loops are large enough to fit over the wire. String them onto the charm holder with any other charms you have chosen.

Fuse the ends of the 14-gauge fine silver into 3 mm balls (p. 103). The final size of this piece is ¾ in. long.

A Gently open the loops on the charm holder and place the bail bar in. Close the loops.

Tie suede or silk cord around the bail bar.

ANDROMEDA CUFF

After attempting to make my own lampworked beads, I gained great respect for glass bead artists. I wanted to design a bold statement that would help display these wonderful creations at their best. The combination of bold wire, beads, and overall size are sure to catch anyone's attention.

BY PAM BROWN

Sizing can be difficult, because the thickness of the beads makes the bracelet stand off the wrist, requiring a wire base that is longer than your actual desired size. Keep this in mind as you work.

Step 1: Form the outside waves

A Cut two 24-in. pieces of 16-gauge wire. Work two wires together to create identical waves. Place the center of the wire in the stepped pliers on the largest barrel and bend the wires up to form a large U. This bend will hold the beads.

B From the base of the U, mark the wires at approximately ⅜ in. (10 mm) on each side.

C Using stepped pliers with the smallest barrel on the outside of the wires, grab the pen mark. Bend the wires down over the pliers. This bend will contain the woven section between the beads.

D Continue the process of bending loops, alternating the small barrel and large one until you have five to six bead loops and four to five weaving loops. (You may choose to make one less of each until you determine the exact length you need.) Repeat on the other end of the wires for a total of 9–11 bead loops and 8–10 weaving loops.

Check the final length of the bracelet and double-check the size of the waves against your beads. You can shrink or expand the waves a bit if you need to, but be sure to change both wires together. This part usually ends up about 7 in. (17.8 cm) for a standard wrist. To help determine the final length of the bracelet and how it fits, you may want to temporarily string in beads, put them into the waves, and tape it together a bit. Gently form it around your wrist without bending it too much. Remember you will be adding about 1 in. (25.5 mm) for the clasp. If you need to add or remove waves, this is a good time to do that. Be aware that once the bracelet is hammered in the next step it becomes harder to manipulate.

E Place the waves so they are mirror images of each other. Use the flat end of a chasing hammer on a steel bench block to slightly flatten the waves only. Use the rounded end of the hammer to add texture. Recheck your length and make final adjustments.

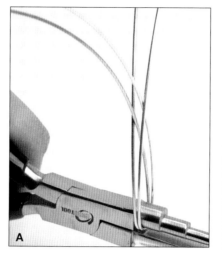

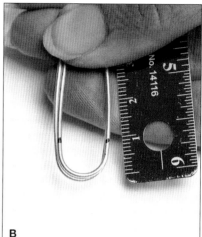

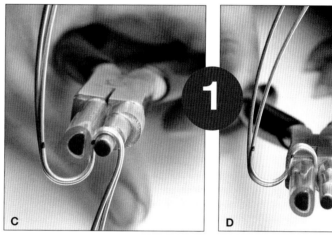

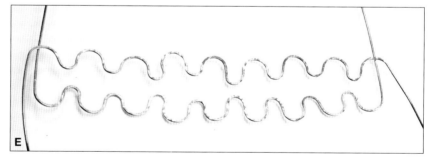

HINTS

Substitute 18-gauge wire for the center wire if your beads don't have a hole large enough for the 16 gauge.

If your bead has a large hole in it, you may want to compensate by stringing seed beads inside or, even better, making some coils to fill the hole and keep the bead centered on the wire.

Another option to change the size of the bracelet is to change the type of clasp. If you need it to be smaller, make simple hook-and-loop closures without the extra wrapping and folded wire.

Step 2: Weave and add beads

Cut a 1-ft. (30.5 cm) piece of 16-gauge wire. String the center bead on the wire and place it between the two middle large waves.

A Cut an 18-in. (45.7 cm) piece of 24-gauge wire. Wrap the wire once around one of the small waves adjacent to the bead, coming over the top of the wave wire, and leaving a small tail you will trim later. Now weave the wire by going under the center wire, over and around the right-hand small wave, back over the center wire, and under and around the left-hand small wave. Repeat until you have as many weaves as desired. Wrap the wire at least one full time around the center wire before continuing.

B Wrap the weaving wire around the center wire to keep the next bead centered in the wave. Add a bead onto the center wire, placing it in the large wave adjacent to the weave just made. Wrap the weaving wire over the bead, and duplicate the same number of wraps made just before the bead on the center wire, and begin your weaving around the small waves as you did in Step 2A. Always alternate weaving over and under the center wire.

Repeat Step 2B, adding wire as needed, and then go back to the center and work in the other direction.

If desired, use chainnose pliers to kink the wire that passes over each lampworked bead (p. 23). Check the size one more time as this is your last chance to make adjustments, but be sure to have at least 4 in. (10.2 cm) of straight wire at the end of each wave wire to construct the clasp.

Step 3: Create the clasp

A After the last wave, wrap the center wire over and around the two straight ends of the wave wire, first wrapping to the left of the center wire, and then crossing under to the right.

Repeat on the other side of the bracelet.

B Make a 90-degree bend in the end of the wave wires approximately ⅛ in. (3 mm) on each side of the wrapped center wire. Repeat on the other side.

C Make hooks on one end by folding each wire inward, creating a ¾ in. (19 mm) piece of doubled wire.

D Wrap each hook wire around the last wave, wrapping toward the wrap made by the center wire. Roll the doubled wire into hooks using roundnose pliers.

E On the other end, using roundnose pliers, form loops that the hooks will fit into about ¼ in. (6.5 mm) above the 90-degree bends, and center the loops over the wires.

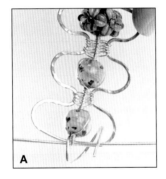

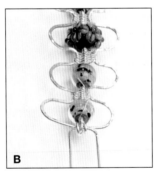

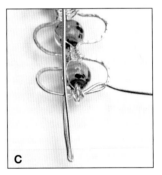

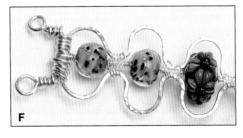

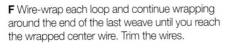

F Wire-wrap each loop and continue wrapping around the end of the last weave until you reach the wrapped center wire. Trim the wires.

Step 4: Form the bracelet

After you have completed the bracelet, you will need to form it into an oval shape very carefully, with your hands. Work it slowly and carefully, being aware of the beads and weaving so you don't put too much stress on any one area. Double-check to make sure the hook and loops work together, making minor adjustments as needed.

Chapter 5 • Chain and Wire

So far, we've worked exclusively with raw wire, meaning wire that has not been manipulated into any type of form. We've been the exclusive creators of its final destiny, the writers of its story. But in this chapter, we'll work with wire that has already taken one step toward becoming something else. Chain and beading wire provide us with an entirely new level of texture and flexibility in creating unique designs. When broken down into their basic components, these two items are made of wire, after all, and by combining them with the raw wire we've already been working with, we'll have a chance to create designs that have incredible complexity and movement.

SPOTLIGHT
Tips and Techniques

About beading wire

In the relatively short time that I have been creating jewelry (in relation to our art's long history, of course), beading wire has come a long way. When stringing, we are no longer stuck with only fibrous materials such as silk that has the potential to warp and break, or thick wires that kink the moment you take your jewelry off. Beading wire today is supple and drapes like a fine thread but has the strength of wire. It is knottable and weavable, yet holds its shape and comes in a variety of diameters, colors. Marketed under such brand names as Softflex and Beadalon, these beading wires all have one thing in common: They are a combination of numerous fine wires bound together in a nylon coating. And in general, the more wires that are inside the nylon coating, the better the wire will drape, and the less likely it will be to kink.

In addition to being labeled with diameter, most fine beading wires have a wire count marked on the package. This can help you determine the best product for your project. For the sake of our projects, we will be looking for high wire counts (49) so we can use the wire for its draping effect. Other beading wires will suffice; you just may find that they kink or lose their shape over time.

About chain

There are hundreds, if not thousands, of styles of chain. Chain offers a textural component to your work, in addition to providing a practical way to finish your pieces and make them wearable. Don't be afraid to combine multiple styles of chain, layering textures. Some of the most common chain styles are pictured at left. A brief description of each follows, beginning at the top of the photo and working down:

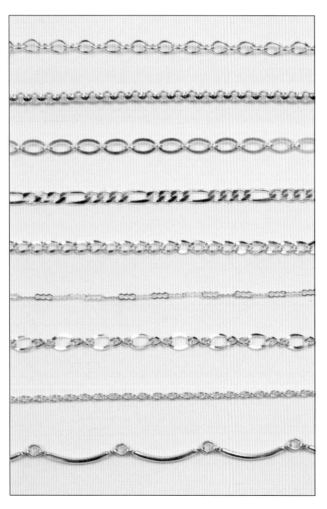

Cable—same-size oval links. When the wire made to use this chain is flattened, its called a flat cable chain. When the ovals are stretched out, almost into a rectangle, it's called a drawn cable chain. Common textures include a corrugated or hammered finish.

Rollo—round links that are all the same size. Generally, these chains are made with half-round wire.

Long and short—a series of long links, whether they be rectangles, diamonds, or ovals, connected together by one or more smaller round or oval links.

Figaro—similar to long and short chains, but the links are flattened to lay flat and face the same direction.

Curb—similar to cable chains, but like figaro chains, they are flattened to lay flat and face the same direction.

Krinkle—similar to drawn cable chains with the exception that the long rectangular links have wavy sides.

Figure 8—a small figure-8 link connected to a larger oval link.

Rope—extremely small links twisted together to resemble a rope.

Bar—straight or curved bars connected by small round links.

Cutting chain

Many of our projects require that you cut lots of chain, or cut chain into equal pieces. One easy way to do this is to measure one piece of chain to the desired length and then count the links. Then each additional piece of chain can be cut by the number of links rather than measuring each one separately. However, when you are using longer pieces of chain, it can be tedious to count the links. In these cases, hang one of the cut pieces from an awl. Then, hang the uncut chain and simply match up the length.

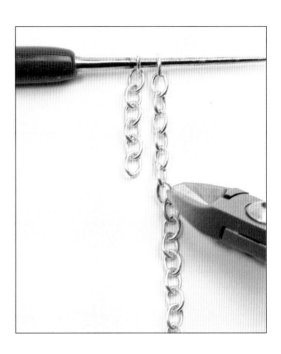

SPOTLIGHT Tools

Crimping pliers might not seem like a standard tool mentioned in a wireworking book; but they not only allow us to incorporate beading wire into our designs, they also have some hidden secrets that can help us make working with wire easier. See Chapter 6 to learn how to use crimping pliers (p. 100). Here, we will discuss other uses for this tool.

But first lets discuss the tool itself. Crimping pliers have two channels, one that is U shaped and one that is an oval, or egg, shaped. The U channel, begins to fold the crimp bead in half, while the oval channel completes the process of completely folding the crimp bead in half, while maintaining a tubular shape. The oval channel is especially useful for other applications. For example, you can use it to tuck in the cut tail of a wire wrap. The circular shape of the indentations in the pliers will protect the shape of the coil on the wire wrap as you squeeze down the cut tail. You can also use it to grasp crimp bead covers. These handy items look like beads that are split down the side. This allows you to slide them over crimp beads, or for that matter anything else you want to hide, and then gently squeeze them closed. Once again, the rounded shape of the pliers allows you to protect the shape of these beads while squeezing them … not to mention keeping them from jumping out of your pliers!

CHAIN AND WIRE EARRING TRIO

My inspiration came from the principles of stringing a bead on beading wire. Think of these simply as strung necklaces in miniature.

Tools
- chainnose pliers and/or flatnose pliers
- crimping pliers
- flush wire cutters
- ruler

BY CORINNA VANKLEECK

Heads Will Turn

On the beading wire, center a 1 in. (25.5 mm) length of decorative chain. Weave a wire end into each link of a 1-in. piece of cable chain, allowing the chain to collapse or scrunch on the wire. Repeat on the other end. String a ½-in. (13 mm) piece of decorative chain on each end.

String the beads as desired. On each end, string one long link of the decorative chain. Insert the beading wire ends into a crimp bead from opposite directions, leaving a ⅛-in. (3 mm) tail. Crimp the crimp bead, trim the wires, and close a crimp cover over the folded crimp. Bring the large single chain links up on each side so they form a pyramid over the crimp cover. Connect the 2½ mm jump ring through the links (to orient the chandelier) forward and attach to the earring wire. Make a second earring.

Materials
- **4** 6 mm rondelle/saucer beads
- **4** 4 mm rondelle/saucer beads
- **4** 3 mm round beads
- **4** 1-in. (25.5 mm) lengths of oval cable chain
- **2** 1-in. (25.5 mm) lengths of decorative chain (short and long links)
- **4** ½-in. (13 mm) lengths of decorative chain (short and long links)
- **4** single long-links of decorative chain (short and long links)
- **2** 2½ mm ID, 20 gauge jump rings (others will work)
- **2** 4-in. (10.2 cm) pieces of beading wire, medium to heavy .014 – .018)
- **2** 2 x 2 mm crimp beads
- **2** 4 mm crimp covers
- pair of earring wires

Basic Skills: BL, WW, EW, JR

Road to Morocco

Materials)
- **2** 4 in. (10.2 cm) pieces beading wire, medium to heavy (approximately .014 to .018)
- **2** 12 mm flat teardrop beads
- **2** 6 mm bicone crystals
- **6** 4 mm bicone crystals
- **6** 3 mm round beads
- **2** 4 mm heishi spacers
- **2** 2 x 2 mm crimp beads
- **2** large crimp covers
- **2** 1½-in. (38 mm) headpins
- **2** 4 mm oval jump rings
- **6** 6 mm oval jump rings
- **4** 8 mm oval jump rings
- **2** 2 in. pieces rollo chain
- **4** 1 in. (25.5 mm) pieces cable chain
- pair of earring wires

Make these to complement the necklace by the same name (p. 86).

On beading wire, string a 3 mm round and the end of a 2-in. (51 mm) piece of rollo chain. String a 4 mm crystal. Weave the beading wire through each link of a 1-in. (25.5 mm) piece of cable chain, allowing it to scrunch. String a 6 mm crystal, 1 in. of scrunched cable chain, and a 4 mm crystal. String the remaining end link of rollo chain and drape in an arc. String a 3 mm round bead.

Insert both ends of the beading wire into a crimp bead from opposite directions leaving a ⅛-in. (3 mm) tail. Crimp the crimp bead, trim the wires, and close a crimp cover over the crimp.

On a headpin, wire-wrap a 4 mm crystal, a heishi spacer, a teardrop bead, and a 3 mm round. Attach the wire-wrapped beads to a 4 mm oval jump ring.

Place a 6 mm oval jump ring on each side of the crimp cover and connect to the 4 mm jump ring on the wire-wrapped component. Place the 8 mm oval jump rings on each side of the 6 mm jump rings and attach them together above the crimp cover with a 6 mm oval jump ring. Attach the jump ring to the earring wire. Make a second earring.

Cascade Waterfall

Make a wire-wrapped linked chain with three beads: Make a wire-wrapped dangle on a headpin and attach to the bead chain. String the end of a 4½-in. (11.4 cm) piece of chain, the end of a 3½-in. (89 mm) piece of chain, a spacer, the wire-wrapped beads, a spacer, the other end of the 3½-in. chain, and the other end of the 4½-in. chain onto a jump ring and hang from an earring wire. Make a second earring.

Materials
- **8** 5 mm rondelle beads
- **4** 4 mm spacers
- **2** 4½-in. (11.4 cm) lengths of small cable chain
- **2** 3½-in. (89 mm) lengths of small cable chain
- **8 in.** 24-gauge wire
- **2** 6 mm ID 18-gauge jump ring
- **2** 1-in. (25.5 mm) headpins
- pair of earring wires

ROAD TO MOROCCO

This simple necklace is a perennial favorite. It's a great way to showcase beautiful semiprecious beads or even lentil-shaped lampworked beads.

WW **JR** **PT**

Materials
- 1 ft. (30.5 cm) 24-gauge wire
- **11** 4 mm oval jump rings
- **4** 1-in. (25.5 mm) lengths of blackened medium cable chain
- **4** 1-in. (25.5 mm) lengths of raw medium cable chain
- **2** 5-in. length of blackened medium cable chain
- **2** 5-in. length of raw medium cable chain
- charm
- 6 mm bicone crystal
- **5** 3 mm round beads
- **9** 4 mm heishi spacers
- **4** 4 mm bicone crystals
- **2** 10 mm oval beads
- 10 x 13 mm teardrop bead
- 20 x 10 mm oval bead
- lobster claw clasp

Tools
- chainnose pliers and/or flatnose pliers
- crimping pliers
- flush wire cutters
- ruler

BY CORINNA VANKLEECK

A Using 24-gauge wire, wire-wrap a 6 mm bicone crystal to a charm of your choice. Add to this a wire-wrapped teardrop bead, heishi spacer, and 3 mm round bead.

B String a 20 x 15 mm oval bead onto a 2-in. (51 mm) piece of 24-gauge wire and make wrapped loops on each end. Pair each 1-in. (25.5 mm) length of darkened chain with a 1-in. length of raw chain. Connect the two pairs together with a jump ring.

C Connect the charm component to the jump ring at the center of the chains. Use jump rings to attach the other ends of the chain to the loops on the oval bead. Use jump rings to attach another 1-in. chain pair to each of the loops on the oval bead.

D Wire-wrap together a 3 mm bead, heishi spacer, 4 mm bicone crystal, heishi spacer, 10 mm oval bead, heishi spacer, 4 mm bicone, heishi spacer, and 3 mm round bead. Repeat. Use jump rings to attach the components to the chain extending from the oval bead.

E Pair each 5-in. (12.7 cm) length of darkened chain with a 5-in. piece of raw chain. Use jump rings to attach them to the multi-bead component. Finish with a lobster claw clasp.

BYGONE ERA

I once spied a necklace rendered in a painting by Alphonse Marie Mucha, my favorite artist of the Pre-Raphaelite and Art Nouveau eras, and instantly knew I must have one! At that time, my personal metal-working skills did not include piercing, soldering, or stone setting so I set to myself the challenge of using the wire-wrapping skills I did have at the time. The result is my version of that coveted medallion Mucha had forever captured in a painting from a bygone era.

Materials

- 39 mm Hill Tribe square link
- **9** 6 mm round beads
- **22** 4 mm round beads
- **18** 4 mm coil spacers
- 15 in. (38.1 cm) drawn cable chain
- 9 in. (22.9 cm) cable chain
- 15 in. small cable chain
- 4 ft. (1.22 m) 22-gauge wire, dead-soft
- 2 ft. (61.0 cm) 24-gauge wire, dead-soft
- **10–12** 4 x 6 mm OD 22-gauge jump rings (other ovals will work)
- **3–4** 1½-in. headpins
- lobster claw clasp and jump ring

Tools

- roundnose pliers
- chainnose pliers
- flatnose pliers
- flush wire cutters
- ruler

BY MELISSA CABLE

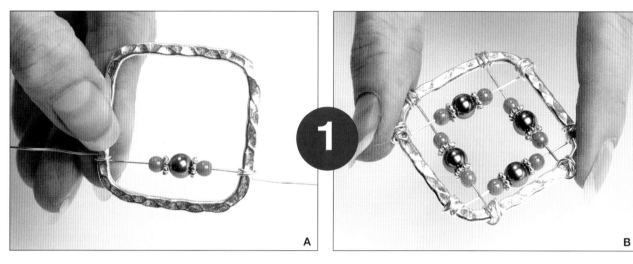

Step 1: Wrap the wire grid

A On the back of the square, center a 6-in. (15.2 cm) piece of 22-gauge dead-soft sterling wire so it's parallel to one side of the square and ¼ in. (6.5 mm) from the inside edge. Wrap one end around the square. String a 4 mm round bead, a spacer, a 6 mm round bead, a spacer, and a 4 mm bead. Wrap the other end around the square. Continue wrapping each end until it's a loose, organic-looking cluster of wraps.

B Repeat Step 1A to wrap the remaining three sides.

Tip
Hill Tribe silver darkens much more slowly than sterling silver does because it doesn't contain copper (the element the liver of sulfer responds to). Patina the square first, unless you want your overall necklace to be really dark.

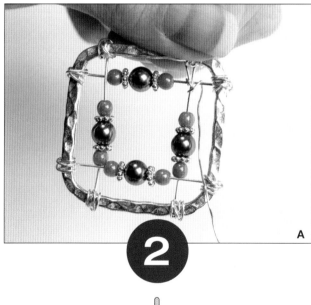

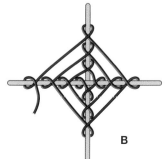

Step 2: The God's eye wrap

Lay a 6-in. (15.2 cm) length of 24-gauge dead-soft sterling-silver wire alongside one of the 22-gauge spokes in the wire grid so it rests on top of a cross wire. Extend a ½-in. (13 mm) tail past the outside of the square frame. Hold it in place with your finger on the backside of the frame.

A Wrap the 24-gauge piece around the 22-gauge spoke, making a full rotation around the wire. Keep your wraps small, snug, and close to the center axis. Now lay the 24-gauge wire over the spoke to the right of the one you just wrapped, and repeat.

B Continue wrapping one spoke at a time in a counterclockwise direction until you've made three wraps around each spoke. Make sure each wrap lies right next to the one before it. This will prevent your God's eye from getting any bigger than ¼ in. If it grows larger than ¼ in., your beads will get too crowded for the frame.

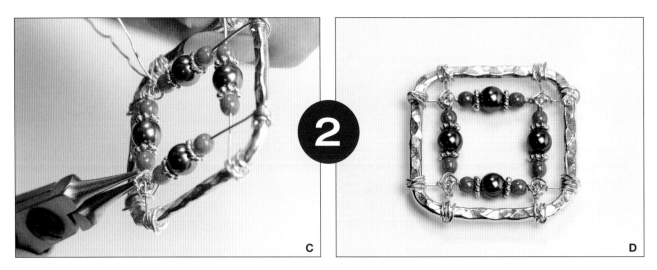

C

D

Step 2: continued

C When you have completed one God's eye, flip your piece over so you are looking at the back. Take a pair of chainnose pliers and twist both tails together so they become one wire. Clip this new tail to ¼ in. and roll the raw end in toward the back of the God's eye wrap with a pair of roundnose pliers.

D Repeat to make a God's eye wrap in each corner so all your beads are nestled into place. Remember this is a very organic piece, nothing will be exact.

Step 3: Add the chain fringe

Take the three different size chains you have picked and plan the length arrangement, picking the center length first. Lay the pieces out before cutting to avoid waste. Stagger five or seven pieces of chain with the longest in the center and with lengths getting shorter as you move outward.

Once you've measured the lengths and have them laid out to your liking, connect them to the pendant accordingly using 4 x 6 mm oval jump rings. Close the jumps rings on the back side of the pendant.

Use headpins to wire-wrap coordinating 4 mm beads to the ends of every other chain.

Step 4: Chain construction

The final step in completing your necklace is to construct the variegated neck chain pieces. You will be staggering different lengths of chain as you go.

Use the two 4 x 6 mm oval jump rings to connect chains to the pendant outside the wraps that anchor the wire grid.

On one side of the pendant, attach a single 1-in. (25.5 mm) length of the drawn cable chain. Attach two ½-in. lengths of the fine cable chain and one ½-in. length of cable chain to the jump ring on the other side.

Use 22-gauge wire to wire-wrap a link made of a 4 mm round, a spacer, a 6 mm round, a spacer, and a 4 mm round to each side of the chain segments.

After wrapping on the beads, continue attaching chain segments, alternating between a single length of the drawn cable chain and three lengths of the smaller cable chains with wrapped beads in between until you have the finished length desired.

Make sure both sides of the necklace are equal in length and attach the clasp to the end.

ARABIAN CUFF

This cuff was inspired by my love of things both whimsical and flavored by Middle Eastern culture. I'm reminded of the elaborate costumes of belly dancers with all the shaker bells and fringe. And although I've not used any bells, I certainly haven't held back on the fringe! It feels wonderful on the wrist and is easily played up or down to suit your personal style.

BY CORINNA VANKLEECK

Step 1: Calculations and cutting

First things first: the prep work! There is a large amount of chain to cut and the project goes much more quickly if you do it beforehand.

The bracelet is made from 1-in. (25.5 mm) long wired sections divided by flat spacer bars. To calculate the total length of the bracelet, add together each section and the width of the spacer bars. So, if you have a 6½-in. (16.5 cm) wrist, plan for a six-section bracelet.

The first and the last chain sections use 12 beads, eight ½-in. (13 mm) lengths of rollo chain, eight ½-in. lengths of cable chain and 16 ½-in. lengths each of figaro and crinkle chains. The remaining chain sections use 12 beads and six ½-in. lengths of rollo chain, six ½-in. lengths of cable chain, and 12 ½-in. lengths each of figaro and crinkle chains.

For a six-section cuff, cut 40 ½-in. lengths of rollo chain, 40 ½-in lengths of cable chain, and 80 ½-in. lengths of figaro and crinkle chains. (Remember that you lose links every time you cut the chain, which is why the materials list calls for more chain than actually used.)

It may be easier to cut the chain to the proper lengths by counting links instead of measuring each piece. A guide to the link count per half inch is below.

7 links	3.5 mm rollo chain
5 links	3.5 mm flat cable chain
3 links	fine figaro chain
5 links	2 mm crinkle chain

Step 2: The frame

Cut the frame wires equal to the length of the chain section calculated in 1A plus 1½ in. (38 mm). The following instructions assume six chain sections for a 6½-in. finished bracelet.

Cut four 7½-in. (19.1 cm) lengths of 16- or 18-gauge wire, depending on what will fit through the 4-strand connectors. If using 18 gauge, gently hammer the lengths with a rawhide hammer on a steel bench block to slightly harden the metal.

Roll a 5 mm loop on both ends of all four wires.

String an end loop into a hole in the four-strand spacer bar and roll closed. Repeat for the remaining loops and holes. In the sample shown, we've used the same two-strand connectors as we used throughout the bracelet, which happen to have center spaces that accommodate the other two bars. Simply use an awl to stretch the holes as needed to fit the wire.

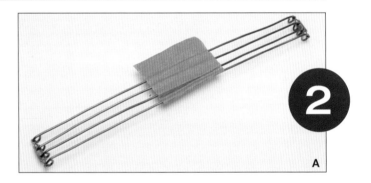

A Use tape to secure each bar 4 mm apart. This will also help to keep the bars straight and better hold the shape of the frame. You can also place a pipe cleaner through the loops on all four wires to keep things sturdy and give you something to hold onto.

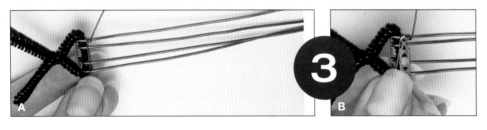

Step 3: Section 1 spacer bar

Work slowly at the beginning, keeping the frame straight and snug and avoiding kinks in the wire. After the first few rows are woven on, the piece has more stability and it gets much easier.

Label each bar and space of the frame: The bar farthest from you is Bar 1, next closest to you is Bar 2, next is Bar 3 and the bar closest to you is Bar 4. The space between B1 and B2 is Space A. The space between B2 and B3 is Space B, and Space C is between B3 and B4 (illustration).

A Cut 3 ft. (91.4 cm) of 24-gauge wire. Holding the fame with the pipe cleaner on the left and the bars extending to the right, wrap the last 2 in. (51 mm) of 24-gauge wire around B1 twice, away from your body and to the right.

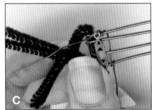

BAR 1	
BAR 2	SPACE A
BAR 3	SPACE B
BAR 4	SPACE C

B Bend the ends of the spacer bar back 45 degrees so it can seat itself over the wires. String the spacer bar onto the 2-in. tail and wrap the tail around B1 twice, going toward the left.

C From the back of the bracelet, bring the long length of 24-gauge wire up through space C and wrap around B4 twice. String the other end of the spacer bar onto the wire and wrap the wire twice around B4, toward the right.

Step 4: Add a chain row

As you wrap the wire around the frame, be sure to wrap toward the right. Whenever you are adding chain, you will be wrapping away from you, going bar to bar from B4 to B1. In the next step when you add beads, you will be wrapping toward you going from B1 to B4.

Each section has seven rows—four bead rows and three chain rows that alternate. However, the first and last sections only have six rows. Section 1 skips the first bead row and the final section skips the last bead row, so the bracelet starts and ends with a chain row.

A With 24-gauge wire, pick up one length of figaro, one rollo, and one crinkle chain. Let these fall down to B4, making sure the chains remain resting on top of the frame and to the side of the wire that is facing space C. Make one wrap around B4, securing the chain.

B From the back, come through space B and wrap around B3 once. Pick up a length of figaro, cable, and crinkle and let them fall to B3. Make one wrap around B3 to secure the chain.

From the back, come through space A and wrap around B2 once. Pick up a length of figaro, rollo, and crinkle and let them fall to B2. Make one wrap around B2, to secure the chain.

From the back come up around the outside of B1 and wrap once around B1. Pick up a length of figaro, a cable, and a crinkle, and let them fall down to B1. Make one wrap around B1, securing the chain.

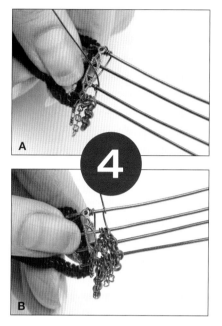

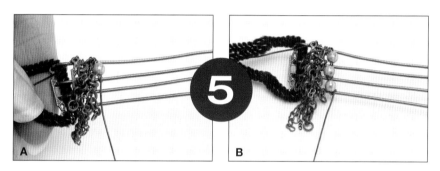

Step 5: Add a bead row

Always push each new row against the previous row to keep everything tight.

A String a bead on the wire and position it into space A. String the wire down through space B and wrap it once around B2.

String a bead on the wire and position it into space B. String the wire down through space C and wrap it once around B3.

B String a bead onto the 24-gauge wire and position it into space B. String your wire around the outside of B4 and secure it to B4 by wrapping it once.

Repeat Steps 4 and 5 until you have four rows of chain and four rows of beads.

Step 6: Start a new section

Using the same 24-gauge wire, string a two-bar spacer onto the frame as in Step 3B and 3C.

Now repeat Steps 5 and 4, starting with Step 5 until you have four rows of beads and three rows of chain.

After two sections, start with a fresh 3 ft. (91.4 cm) piece of wire, as you did in Step 3 and then repeat Steps 6A and 6B until you have five sections strung. You can also remove the tape at this time.

In the final section, finish with a row of chain, skipping the last row of beads.

Step 7: Finish the cuff

Create loops on the end of the wire and connect to the four-strand spacer bar in the same manner as Step 2.

Wire-wrap a bead to the end of every rollo and every cable chain that is secured to B1 and B4.

Gently, but firmly, bend the cuff into its proper shape.

Hints
Add a clasp if you'd like. For example, on one end of the frame, string a large lobster claw on a jump ring over the space bar between B2 and B3. On the second end of the frame, string a large linked chain between B2 and B3 for the lobster claw to grasp. You can attach a hook-and-eye clasp the same way.

CRISTINA'S CUFF

Materials
- 18 in. (45.7 cm). 2–3 mm curb or cable chain
- 12 ft. 22-gauge dead-soft or fine wire cut into 3-ft. (91.4 cm) sections
- 3 ft. 22-gauge or 24-gauge dead-soft or fine wire
- **4** 2.5 mm 20-gauge ID jump rings
- approx. **60** 3–6 mm beads
- clasp of your choice
- 6 in. (15.2 cm) craft wire

Tools
- beading loom
- chainnose pliers
- roundnose pliers
- wire cutters

One of my favorite projects was a bracelet called Rock Candy by Cristina Hererra. Cristina was a classically trained jeweler, but her true love was experimentation. She always found innovative ways to use the tools and supplies that surrounded her, such as using a bead loom to hold strands of chain so she could stitch beads back and forth between the links. This bracelet, in her memory, combines her loom technique with my love of freeform wire weaving.

BY MELISSA CABLE

Step 1: Prepare the loom

A Wire the ends of the chain together with the craft wire, leaving a 1-in. (25.5 mm) piece of wire between them.

B Loop the chain around the pegs on the dowels located on both ends of the loom, positioning the chain to reflect the width you desire for your cuff.

Tighten the chain by loosening the wing nuts on the dowels and rotating the dowel so it pulls the chain tighter. Adjust one end at a time and retighten the wing nut when you have good tension.

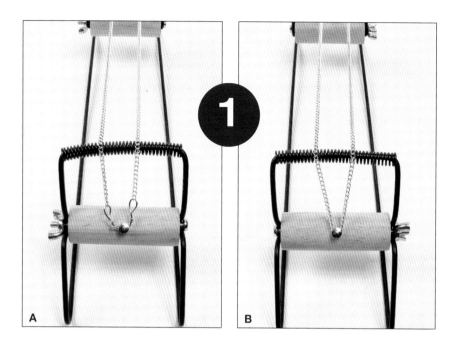

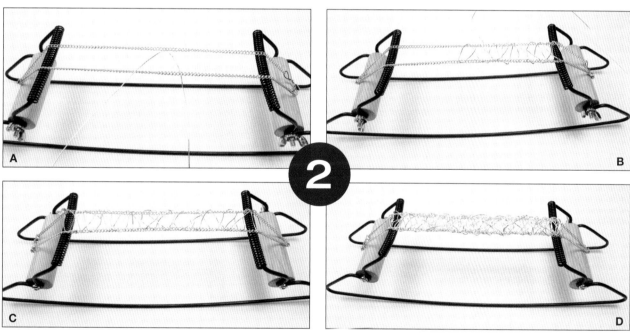

Step 2: Begin weaving the wire

I will often place a large bench block across the legs of the loom to keep it from sliding around as I work.

A Take one 3-ft. (91.4 cm).section of 22-gauge wire and string it halfway through any chain link.

B Pull one end of the wire across the top of the chains and string it into a link on the opposite side. Pull the wire across the top of the chains again and string it into a link on the opposite side. Do this randomly, always going over the top of the chain and trying not to pass the wire at a distance longer than 1¼ in. (32 mm) of wire. The goal of this first wire is to set the distance between the chains, so try not to pull too tightly as you go. When you have finished with that end of the wire, wrap it around the chain once or twice and trim.

C Repeat with the other side of the wire, trying to cover the space between the chains evenly. Wrap the wire around the chain twice to anchor it, trying to make sure you pick a spot away from the place you ended the last wire.

D Repeat Steps 2A–C with the remaining three 22-gauge 3-ft. wire sections, loading and weaving as you did with the first one. If you run out of chain links (which depends on how big your chain is and how many passes you do between the chains), simply insert the wire between a previous weave and the chain.

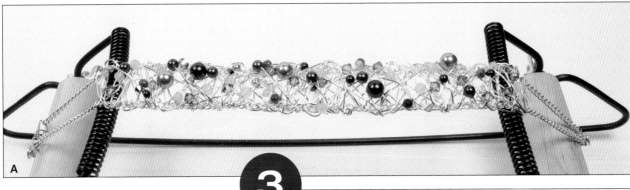

Step 3: Load the beads and embellish the wire

You can use 22-or 24-gauge wire for this step, depending on the hole size of the beads you choose.

A Repeat Steps 2A–C, but load 1–3 beads on the wire during each pass. Don't be too worried about how the beads are positioned; you will slide them around a little at the end. However, when you cross a wire over a wire that contains beads, make sure the beads are approximately where you want them as the crossing wire will lock them into place and prevent further movement.

B Once all the beads are loaded, use roundnose pliers to gently place kinks on every wire (p. 23). You can use this as a way to separate the beads and keep them in place.

Notice that as you kink the wire, it often reveals the layer of wire below. Be sure to kink the wires below the surface layers when possible to achieve a uniform look. You can even turn the piece over and kink from the bottom. If any wires stick out from the sides further than they should, you can kink the wire and loop it toward the face of the bracelet to help achieve a uniform edge on your bracelet.

Step 4: Add the clasp

Remove the bracelet from the loom by loosening the dowels on each end of the loom, and gently curve the bracelet to fit your wrist.

Trim the chains to the desired length and link a jump ring between them on each side, creating a "V" shape. Attach a clasp to these jump rings as desired, or wire-wrap a bead between the jump ring and clasp if you need more length.

Chapter 6 • Basics

Here's a quick page reference for all the basic techniques explained in Chapter 6.

BASICS

CT Cutting

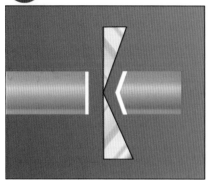

Wire cutters are perhaps the most important tool to learn how to use properly when working with wire. Learning how to create a flush cut, meaning a cut that leaves a blunt wire rather than a pointed piece of wire, is extremely important, both in creating a quality piece and for creating a comfortable piece that does not poke you.

Tools
• wire cutters

Your wire cutters have two sides. One side has a well. When you place the wire into the wire cutters from this side and cut, the wire will have a pointed end. The other side of the cutters has a flat surface. When you place the wire into the cutters from this side, the end will be flush. How flush the cut will be depends greatly on what type of wire cutters you have. Look for flush cutters when buying wire cutters. If you invest in one good tool, you'll be glad you chose quality wire cutters.

BL Basic Loops

Tools
• roundnose pliers (graduated or stepped)
• chainnose pliers
• wire cutters

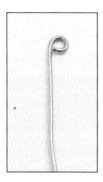 

Round loops
Start at the very end of your wire. If you start further down from the end, you will have a straight piece of wire on the inside of your loop, likely turning your loop into a teardrop (pictured at right).

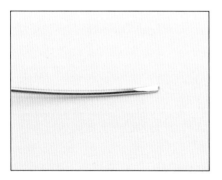 

Tight loops
Slightly flatten the end of the wire using chainnose pliers or a chasing hammer and steel bench block. Start a loop and then use chainnose pliers to squeeze it closed.

Centered loops
After creating a loop, place one barrel of roundnose pliers back into the loop, and grasp the wire at the point where the circle closes. Bend the circle backwards 45 to 60 degrees.

Wire-wrapping

Perfect wire-wraps, every time

After teaching hundreds of wire-wrapping classes, I have developed The Five C's of Wire-wrapping:

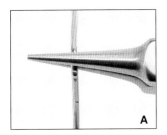

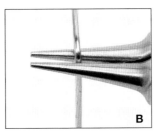

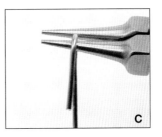

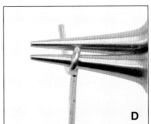

❶ Circle

There are two types of movements when starting a wrapped loop: a pliers movement and a wire movement. Try never to move both at the same time. You will start by alternating between pliers and wire movements.

A Roundnose pliers: Hold parallel to the table in your natural hand.
Wire: Point to the ceiling.
Roundnose pliers: Grasp the wire 1 in. (25.5 mm) from the end.

B Wire: Push back 90 degrees, away from you.

Note: if you have a bead on the wire, always grasp the wire directly above the bead. The pliers hold the space you will wrap in. If you leave space between the pliers and the bead, you will end up with too many wraps, making your loop more likely to bend above the bead.

C Roundnose pliers: Ungrip wire, roll in place away from you 45 to 60 degrees. Regrip wire.
Wire: Guide over the top of the pliers back toward you until pointing down at the table.
Roundnose pliers: Ungrip wire, roll in place toward you 45 to 60 degrees, back to its original position. Regrip wire.

D Wire: Push under and away from you on the tip side of the pliers until pointing straight back.

❷ Connect

String the tail of the loop into the item you wish to connect (for example, a clasp, a piece of chain, another wrapped loop). Pull gently until the item settles itself into the circle you created in Step 1.

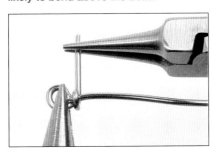

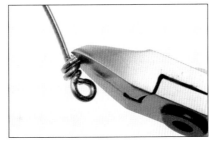

❸ Coiling (Wrap)

Hold the chainnose pliers in your left hand, pointing to the ceiling.

Hold the circle you just made so the loop points to the pliers and the wire tail you will be wrapping points to the ceiling. Grip the circle with chainnose pliers.

Use the tip of roundnose pliers to grab the tip of the wire and wrap toward you, releasing and rotating your pliers every wrap so the wire does not become tangled around the pliers. Wrap 2–3 times.

❹ Cover and Cut

This step used to just be cut, but to reinforce the safety aspect of this step I have added the word cover. This reminds you that, before you cut, always hold the tail you are cutting off or position the wire cutter and then cover the piece with your hand before you cut. The end of the wire will often fly, and if you are not wearing safety glasses, it can be a safety hazard for you and your beading buddy's eyes.

To create a clean cut, place the flush side of your cutter against the coil you just created as you grab the end of the wire, cover, and cut.

❺ Clean

Over time you will learn to cut the tail so closely that you'll almost be able to skip this step. But until then, or if you have a hard time seeing the end of the wire when you cut, you will need to take chainnose pliers and gently push the end of the wire in line with the coil. Don't think of it as squeezing the wire end down—this almost always results in a misshapen coil. Instead think that you are gently nudging it down from behind. You can also use crimp pliers in this step. The rounded channel helps protect the shape of the coil as you squeeze the raw end of the wire down.

BASICS

CR Crimping

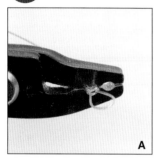

A

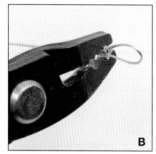

B

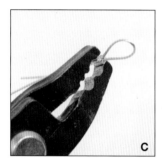

C

Tools
- crimping pliers

Create tight crimp beads

Crimping pliers have two channels. The back one looks like a U and the front channel like an egg.

A Place the crimp bead in the back channel and close the pliers tightly. This will result in a U-shaped crimp bead.

B Now, turn the U-shape 90 degrees so it resembles a C. Place the C into the front channel of the crimp pliers and squeeze again. This will close the C, creating a tube.

C Now, as an extra precaution, you will notice that the end of your crimping pliers have a slightly flat area where the tips of the pliers meet. Before completely removing the crimp bead from the pliers, slide the crimp out between these flat tips and squeeze very lightly. You don't want to misshape the crimp; you just want to make sure the crimp has actually closed completely.

FL Filing

Proper technique

Files remove metal and refine your shape. It is important to remember that you only remove metal on the upward stroke. Therefore, it is important to always go in one direction, lifting your file after each stroke, rather than going back and forth. Going back and forth is not only a waste of your efforts, but will dull your files over time. You should also use a lubricant such as Cut Lube to allow for a smoother movement while filing and to extend the life of your files.

Tools
- metal files
- emery boards
- file lubricant

FINDINGS

🔵 JR Jump Rings

There is often much confusion surrounding Inner Diameter (ID) and Outer Diameter (OD) when it comes to jump rings. Inner diameter is simply the diameter of the dowel that the jump ring was created on. Outer diameter is the combination of the dowel diameter and the wire diameter. You will find a lot of variation in how suppliers label their jump rings. The most important thing to remember is that jump ring size consists of two variables: dowel diameter and wire diameter, usually in millimeters. But no worries—if a project calls for an ID ring and your local store labels them in OD dimensions, use these handy formulas to help you convert the rings to the closest match.

> 22 g = 0.63 mm
> 20 g = 0.81 mm
> 18 g = 1.02 mm
> 16 g = 1.3 mm
> 14 g = 1.63 mm

Converting ID to OD = (wire mm X 2 plus dowel size).

For example, a 18-gauge 3.5 mm ID ring is approximately an 18-gauge 5.5 OD ring (1.02 mm X 2 plus 3.5 mm).

However, keep in mind this doesn't mean that any 5.5 OD ring will work. For example, a 16-gauge wire wrapped on a 3 mm dowel also will yield a 5.5 OD (1.3 mm X 2 plus 3 mm), so the hole size of that ring will be smaller since it is made on a 3 mm dowel, and therefore, may not be large enough for the project's required use. Be sure to always use the correct gauge jump ring specified in the project.

Converting OD to ID = (OD minus wire mm X 2)

For example, a 20-gauge 4 mm OD ring would be equivalent to a 20-gauge 2.4 mm ID (4 mm minus .81 mm X 2).

Notice in the above examples: All jump rings are labeled with a gauge and inner or outer diameter, again, recognizing the importance of both factors in sizing jump rings.

Gauge millimeter equivalents were taken from Tim McCreight's Metalsmith Suite app, available for the iPhone on Apple's app store.

Make jump rings

Determine the size of the wire and size of the dowel you want to use to create your jump ring. Remember that inner diameter (ID) measurements refer to the size of the dowel, outer diameter (OD) measurements refer to the dowel size PLUS the width of the wire on both sides of the ring.

Coil the wire around the dowel, making sure to make more coils than you need rings as you will lose some of them during the cutting process.

A Remove the coil and flush-cut one end.

B Now, flip your wire cutters over and create a flush cut on the next ring, so once it is cut, this end will close precisely with the first flush-cut you made.

Flush-cut the end of the wire again, flip the pliers, and cut the next ring so the end will match up with the flush-cut you just made. Repeat until all your rings are cut.

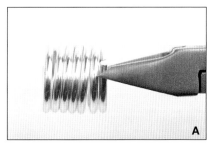

A

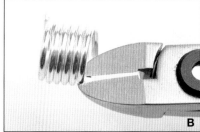

B

Open and close jump rings

The trick to opening and closing jump rings is to never pull the opening outward; always move back and forth. This not only protects the shape of the jump ring, but as you move it forward and back, the joint at the bottom of the ring (directly across from the cut) is getting harder and will therefore resist opening.

Hold the jump ring in chainnose or flatnose pliers so the opening is facing upwards.

C Use another pair of chainnose or flatnose pliers to grab the ring on the other side of the opening and push that side of the rings forward or pull it back.

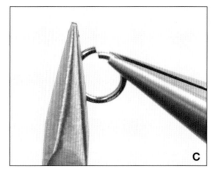

C

Close in the same manner. You can use SLIGHT inward pressure as you go back and forth, waiting for the two ends of the ring to just graze each other as they pass, knowing there is no gap between them.

FINDINGS

Clasps

S-clasps

S-clasps are a great basic clasp that you can easily customize to any size you desire. How big the clasp ends up is determined not only by how long a piece of wire you start with, but where you work on roundnose pliers and how far down you bend the loops. Play with different combinations to discover how altering any of these variables changes the clasp. A jump ring makes a good ending for you to hook into.

A Cut 2½ in. (64 mm) of 16-gauge wire or whatever is called for in your project instructions. Create a tight loop, as described above on each end, but going in opposite directions.

B Hold wire, pliers parallel to the table, ¼ in. (6.5 mm) down from the loop. With the loop facing to the left, roll the wire to the right until the loop nearly comes in contact with the wire.

Repeat on the other end of the wire.

C You can hammer and distress this link as well. One end will remain permanently closed and the other more open to act as the hook.

Tools
- roundnose or bail making pliers
- chainnose pliers
- wire cutters

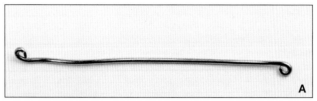

Hook Clasps

A Hook clasps are basically one sided S-clasps. Use the steps above, except instead of creating a loop on both sides of the clasp, make a wrapped loop on one end of the wire. Be sure to connect the loop to your piece before coiling it.

Earring wires

Tools
- roundnose pliers
- chainnose pliers
- ballpoint pen with a cap

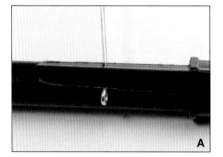

Consistent French earring wires

This trick was shared by my friend and jewelry artist Cristina Hererra, and I have used it ever since.

Start by placing a small loop at the bottom of a 1½ in. (38 mm) piece of 20-gauge half-hard wire.

A Place the wire underneath the cap of a pen, with the loop pulled up against the cap peg, to hold it into place. Be sure the cut end of the loop is facing the pen.

B Roll the wire around the pen, until it nearly passes the loop. Remove the cap, and slide the earring wire off the pen. Use a file or emery board to debur the end of the wire if needed.

Trim the earring wire to the desired length and use chainnose pliers to place a slight bend in the end of the wire.

C Use a chasing hammer and steel bench block to very lightly hammer the wire just above the loop, before you reach the rounded part that goes into your ear.

Note: If you can find the ballpoint pens that have the grooved rubber grips on them, the rubber grooves are a perfect place to nestle your wire as you are wrapping it around the pen.

 **Fused Pins**

Create headpins

This technique works best with fine or sterling silver wire. However, copper will also fuse nicely. Do not try this with base metals. Anytime you heat metals to this point, fumes are released and metals that are not pure, like pure (fine) silver and copper, may have metals in them that produce noxious fumes. This process can be easier to do in dim light so you can better see the flame.

Start your butane torch as directed by the manufacturer. Locate the smaller blue flame that extends directly from the tip of the torch. The flame beyond that turns nearly clear.

A Hold your wire in the middle with cross-locking tweezers. Hold the end of the wire at the tip of the blue flame. As the metal melts, slowly move the wire down, keeping the ball in a consistent place until it is the desired size.

Quench the wire in water to cool it.

Note: Sometimes, larger-gauge wires can take a while to fuse. This is a result of the heat being pulled through the wire and into the cross-locking tweezers (the pliers are acting as a heat sink; they pull the heat away from the object you are heating). You can sometimes speed the process by heating the entire wire, including the tips of the cross-locking tweezers, by moving the piece back and forth through the flame and then concentrating on the end of the wire you want to fuse.

Creating two-sided balled pins: Create in the exact same way as described above, except after fusing your first ball, remove the wire from the flame slowly, giving it just a second to set, and then immediately turn the wire over and fuse the other side. Since the wire and cross-locking tweezer will still be hot, you will find that the second side generally fuses faster.

Some safety notes:
Never hold your wire with your fingers, the wire gets extremely hot very fast and you will suffer a serious burn.

Always tie back your hair, roll up your sleeves, and wear safety glasses.

Never use your pliers to hold the wire. The heat will anneal the tips of the pliers and in no time you will find yourself with pliers that do not meet up at the end.

Move slowly; quick movements with the metal while it is in the heat can cause the ball to drop off or misshape.

Always work over a fireproof surface and follow manufacturer recommendations for filling your torch.

Tools
- butane torch
- cross-locking tweezers with protective grip
- bowl of water

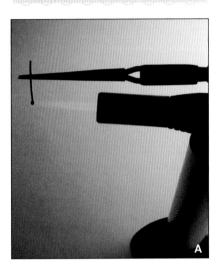

A

FINISHES

Textures

HM Hammered textures

How to hold a hammer: Although any good jeweler will tell you the proper way to hold a hammer is at the end (giving the most efficient use of your swing) I have found that beginners often struggle with achieving their desired results when hammering "properly." With this in mind, I suggest that while you are getting comfortable with your tools, you choose between what I call a force hold or a precision hold, depending on your desired results. To flatten metal, choose a force hold: Grip the hammer at the end, giving the longest extension, and therefore, the most force. To create textures and control how texture is applied, choose a precision hold: Hold the hammer just a little closer to the head, allowing better control and direction.

How to strike metal: Just as there are two ways to hold a hammer, there are two ways to strike metal. To simply harden the metal without spreading it, a straight up and down action is called for. To spread the metal, hammer in an L or J motion while rotating your piece, pulling out as you strike down. It takes some practice, but once you get this skill down, you'll notice a tremendous difference between the two strikes.

How to choose a bench block: A steel bench block is the surface that holds the piece you are hammering. Steel bench blocks are traditionally used for flattening and texturing metal. They come in many sizes and thicknesses. When it comes to blocks, I prefer to buy one good one rather than inexpensive ones that mar easily (thereby transferring their imperfections to your metal) or have a horrible ping to them as you hammer (which I have found is more prevalent in larger, thinner blocks). Reduce the pinging noise, and noise in general, by placing the block on a leather sand- or shot-filled bag. You may also want to consider wearing safety glasses and earplugs for your safety when working extensively with hammers. An alternative to steel bench blocks, rubber bench blocks give when you strike the metal, allowing you to shape your metal as you hammer it. They are inexpensive and also provide a good surface to hold things while you are filing. Although not called for in this book, the rubber bench block is one of my favorite tools.

Hammered with a chasing hammer

Hammered with the flat end of a riveting hammer

Stamped with nail sets

Stamped with nail sets and a screwdriver

Create a hammered finish: Use the rounded side of a chasing hammer, held with a precision hold. Hammer straight up and down to create divots. Don't neglect the edges of the piece, but try not to hammer too hard on the edge, or you risk creating thin, sharp points in your metal that will distort the shape or have to be filed off. Use the flat end of a riveting hammer to create an entirely different hammered texture.

Create a stamped finish: Don't use a chasing hammer for a stamped finish, as the end of the stamp can damage the surface of the chasing hammer. (Keeping the surface of the chasing hammer clean keeps it from marring your metal.) Instead, use a regular household hammer to strike metal stamps, or better yet, try a brass deadblow hammer. For texturing, choose from traditional metal stamps, available in all sort of designs, letters and numbers, and alternatives, such as simple nail sets. Introduced to me by jewelry artist Robert Dancik several years ago, nail sets generally come in a pack of three and allow you to stamp tidy circles of varying sizes. I am also fond of using regular flathead screwdrivers and chisels to create stamped straight lines. Simply set the stamp on the metal and strike it with a household hammer. How hard you hit the stamp will determine how deep the depression is. Be careful—you can actually cut through metal with stamps and screwdrivers if you strike hard enough on thinner gauges.

Bur Textures

To create stardust and satin finishes: This is a subject unto itself. There are many, many burs out there that produce different textures on metals, but for the sake of this book, I will concentrate on two: flame-shaped diamond burs and texture brushes. The reason I like these two burs is that they fit in the head of my cordless bead reamer, making it easy to throw in my bead bag for classes.

The diamond bur creates a stardust texture on metal, while the brush creates a satin finish. When I use the diamond bur, I work across the metal in a circular fashion using the side of the bur. When I use the brush, I try to go in one consistent direction. Both burs work especially well on strip wire, giving even more texture options.

Tools
- handheld tool such as a Dremel or cordless bead reamer, diamond burs, texturing wheel, bur

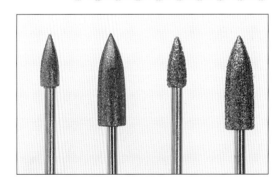

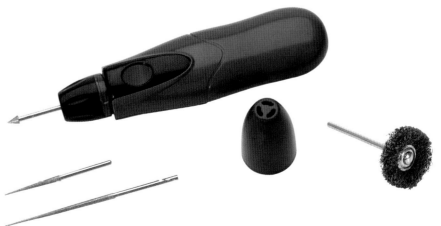

FINISHES

PT Patinas

Add color to metal

Create an antiqued (blackened) patina: Liver of sulfur works on both copper and silver to create a blackened finish that can then be polished back to reveal highlights of polished metal and low-lights of black detail. It is especially useful for pieces that are textured, as it makes the textures stand out. In addition to providing black finishes, liver of sulfur can be used to create finishes that go anywhere from bronze and green to blue and purple. Achieving color takes some practice and it has a lot to do with the temperature of your metal and the liver of sulfur solution, and is sometimes enhanced by the addition of other chemicals. For the sake of this book, we'll discuss blackened finishes only.

Liver of sulfur comes in solid, liquid, and gel form. Each has its own advantages and disadvantages but it's basically the same product. Follow the manufacturers directions for mixing the solution you choose.

I find that I can bring my pieces to black faster by not only having a hot solution, but by running my metal under hot water as well. Once the piece is hot, I place it in the solution either using a small steel basket or by dangling it on a piece of wire. Once it has turned black, rinse it well to stop the reaction and to remove the excess solution. Use steel wool or polishing pads to remove the dark surface, while leaving black in the crevices of your texture.

Whenever you start a project, think about what you want antiqued and plan for it. Oftentimes, you may want to add patina to your wire before working with it; other times, you may want the more intense contrast achieved by antiquing the project at the end and then polishing it.

There are alternative ways to achieve black accents on your metal that do not require the use of liver of sulfur. First, you can apply an alcohol ink to the metal and then polish off the ink on the surface, leaving the black details inside your texture. I use a baby wipe to gently wipe off the excess ink while it is still wet, making the polishing go a little faster. Sharpie pens and Copic markers are two examples of alcohol inks. Adirondack alcohol inks come in bottles and I will often apply them with a foam eye-makeup applicator. Keep in mind, however, that while alcohol inks have good permanency, alcohol products such as perfume and hair spray can remove them or make them run.

Finally, there is the egg method. This is one of the first methods I ever used to antique metal, and in all honesty, I can't remember where I learned it (I would love to credit the clever individual who shared this secret). It relies on the fact that eggs have sulfur in them. And it's simple. Hard boil an older egg and, while it is still hot, crack it and cut it in half. Put the egg, including the shell, into a zip-top plastic bag with your piece and let it sit. You can watch it over the next few hours to see when it has reached the desired level of black. This method takes longer and the results are not always consistent (as you can imagine, sulfur levels in eggs vary greatly), but it is a great non-toxic alternative and a good way to use up those old eggs.

Tools
- liver of sulfur
- butane torch

 **Sanding**

Using sandpapers

Sandpapers are used to remove surface imperfections and to polish the metal. A good jeweler will be able to get a beautiful mirror finish just by using a strong arm and a set of polishing papers.

Whenever you use sandpapers, you will start with the coarsest grit (the smallest number, such as 400) and work your way to the finer grits (larger numbers, such as 1200). The most important thing to remember when sanding is to always rotate your piece or the direction you are sanding by 45 degrees every time you change the grit. If you do not, you will simply be making deeper and deeper grooves in your metal with your sandpaper. By rotating the piece, you are slowly pressing the metal over, into the previous grooves, creating a smoother and smoother surface as you go.

Tools
• sandpaper
• polishing papers

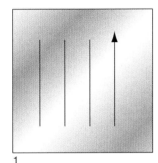

1

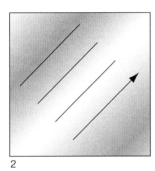

2

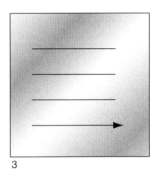

3

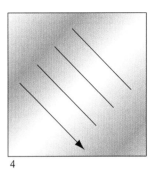

4

CORDS

While there are a variety of commercially produced chain and cords available to display the pendants you created, part of the charm of your finished piece is creating your own cords. Here are four simple ways to make your pieces wearable. Where appropriate, a recommended cord is noted in each project.

CH Convertible Chain

My favorite way to display pendant and large focal pieces is to create a convertible chain that you can wear long or short. To achieve this, attach your pendant to the toggle itself, not its small loop. I start with a 32-in. (81.3 cm) piece of chain.

A Add a jump ring onto the small loop on the toggle bar and string it over the chain.

B Attach the chain ends to the small loop on the toggle ring.

C When you want to wear the piece long, simply slide the toggle bar down to the ring, and connect it through the toggle ring from behind, giving it the appearance of being a front-facing clasp.

D, E, F When you want to wear it short, slide the toggle bar to the middle of the chain, doubling the chain, and then attach it to the toggle from behind, in the same manner as above.

This design works great with rope chain, but almost any chain that will allow the toggle bar to slide easily across it will work.

A

B

C

D

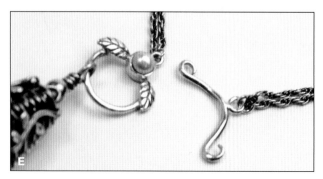

E

F

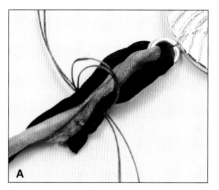

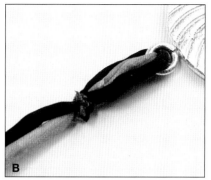

 **Silk Cord**

This technique for ending silk cord works with one or multiple strands.

A Loop the end(s) of the silk through the clasp and stitch the loop closed using a needle and thread. When you stitch it closed, it is best to always bring your needle up from one side, starting your next stitch by going around the sides of the silk and then back up through the silk. This allows you to pull the silk tightly together.

B Tie the ends of the thread together and trim the excess silk.

C Now, simply use a large crimp cover (that matches your clasp) to cover the stitches.

Unless you are using a bail or jump ring that can be opened, be sure to string your pendant on before sewing on the second side.

 **Suede Cord**

There are two ways to end suede cords. The first way is described in the Urban Grace project in Chapter 1. It involves piercing the cord, creating a wrapped loop that attaches your clasp, and then creating an organic coil of wire. I prefer this type of cord for any pendant that will move around on the suede.

Knotted Suede Cord

This cord closure works well for suede cords that are knotted to the pendant, such as the Charming Story pendant. The coiled and balled endings on this cord is pretty, but it can be uncomfortable if used on a cord that might flip over, allowing the balled ends to rub up against your neck. When knotted to the pendants, the cord always remains upright, making the balled ends a pretty touch without compromising the comfort. This cord works well with an S-clasp, but you can add any clasp into the suede loop at the start of Step C.

Cut your suede 2 in. (51 mm) longer than your finished size, not including the clasp. Fold the last inch of each end into a loop. Use an awl to pierce the loop ⅛ in. (3 mm) from the end of the suede.

A Use the fused headpin method described in this chapter to create a balled headpin on a 3-in. (76 mm) piece of 24-gauge fine silver. String the balled headpin through the holes pierced by the awl. Holding the suede firmly in your hand, and the headpin in your cross-locking tweezers, fuse a ball on the other end of the wire. Be sure to NOT touch the wire as you are fusing, as it will be hot. Also be sure the suede is out of the way and there is no risk it will fall into the flame and catch fire.

B String the headpin all the way through and stop just before one of the balls rests on the suede. Bend the headpin back up against the loop. Halfway up the loop, begin wrapping down, toward the other ball.

C When you reach the other ball, twist the two balls together twice and adjust as desired.

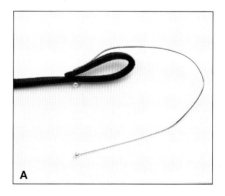

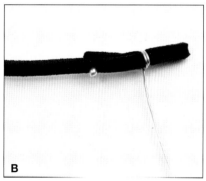

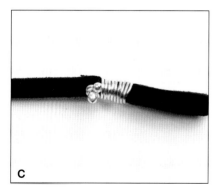

ABOUT THE ARTISTS

Melissa Cable

Melissa Cable has been creating jewelry for over 10 years. Seven of those years, she owned beadclub bead store in Woodinville, Wash. where she quickly recognized her passion for creating and teaching projects that allow her students to learn sound skills while walking away with a fun, finished project. Having satisfied her sense of taste and smell by working in the restaurant and wine industries, she found that creating jewelry satisfies her senses of sight and touch. Combined with the sound of happy students, jewelry making leaves her complete. She has taught at bead stores and shows around the country, and her work is regularly published in magazines and books. *Spotlight on Wire* is her first book. When she is not chasing after her young daughter and son, she might be found writing, running or rambling.

This book is dedicated to Gwyneth and Aiden. This is what happens when you wish upon a star…

Thank you to the former customers of beadclub for all of the friendship, inspiration and support. And no small-business owner could be more lucky or proud to have such an amazing staff—thank you Bonnie (a.k.a. mom), Pam, Cristina, Dawn, Jodi, Sheri, Corinna, Joel, Sharon, Elise, Tammi, Meghan, Ursula, Dale & Rhonda, Courtney, Mary, and Irene. Randi, Kendra, and Robert are owed my deepest appreciation for urging me on in this and other artistic endeavors. I'm lucky to call each of you my mentor and friend. To the Pizzos and the Popolis, my thanks for building more Ikea furniture than you ever thought existed and for putting up with missed dinner dates and vacations. And finally, thank you to the entire Cable clan, especially my husband Chris, who have always loved and supported me no matter what.

Pam Brown

Making jewelry in one form or another since the early 90s, Pam feels very lucky to be able to take all she has learned and share it with others. She began her teaching career while working for Melissa. There she was able to use her broad background in off-loom bead weaving, wire, stringing, and chain mail to help teach a wide variety of classes. She eventually moved into metalwork, and now thoroughly enjoys each medium. Teaching is such a wonderful way to enhance others' lives and she feels very honored to have been able to teach and learn from so many exceptional students. Since beginning her teaching career, Pam has been privileged to teach at the Bead&Button and the Bead Fest shows, appear on *Beads Baubles and Jewels* television show, and be published in beading magazines and books.

I am very thankful for the opportunity to participate in this book. Melissa has been an incredible mentor and friend throughout my teaching career, and the friendships that have been formed through the wonderful atmosphere at the bead store will last a lifetime. I wish to thank all the friends that have been there to pull me through, and all of the students that have helped me become a better teacher. I am also very thankful to my children for putting up with a missing mom and a craft room they can't walk through.

Corinna VanKleeck

From a very early age, Corinna has had a great love for the divine beauty that is in nature. Texture, movement, and color are her vices, and she has never not been working with her hands. She can always also be found playing with puzzles and figuring out how it all fits together. And although she's always got some kind of found object or refurbishing project going on, she has only been designing and creating beaded and wrapped wire jewelry for five years. Sharing the knowledge and skills she has gained is not only a great pleasure and therapy for her, but also a rich reward. It has been an honor and a privilege for her to teach these last four years with Melissa. She has been so greatly challenged and inspired by her wonderful and talented students, colleagues and friends. May the journey only continue.

It is said, that "God gives you the desires of your heart. Then, God gives you the desires of your heart." Thank you Father. My beloved Papa, I thank you too. For always reminding me, just where I need to be. To my dearest Ky, I can't say thanks enough for your loving support and for giving me the freedom to pursue my dreams! And where would I be without the many talented students and extraordinary friends who have inspired and challenged me so greatly? I am deeply grateful for Melissa, and for being so warmly and securely feathered into the beadclub nest, where my journey truly began. This opportunity would never have been possible without you.

RESOURCES

As a former bead store owner, I can't urge you enough to support your local bead and jewelry supply stores. However, as a teacher, I recognize that without the proper tools and supplies, your creative endeavors can be limited. So I have compiled a list of resources for those harder-to-find items. Not all of these resources sell directly, so please visit their websites to find a dealer near you.

Rio Grande
riogrande.com
Silver and copper round and strip wire, tools

Eurotool
eurotool.com
Tool distributor and manufacturer

Softflex Company
softflexcompany.com
Beading wire and craft wire

Somerset Silver
somerset-silver.com
Sterling and Hill Tribe silver

Vintaj
vintaj.com
Natural brass components, charms, and chain

Metalliferous
metalliferous.com
Brass texture plates, wire

Melissa Cable
melissacable.com
Tools, strip wire, brass texture plates, Faux Bone, and free project sheets

International Society of Glass Beadmakers
ISGB.org
Find a local chapter of lampwork artists in your area

Unicorne Beads
unicornebeads.com
Handmade lampworked beads

Grace Ma
gracebeads.com
Handmade lampworked beads

Ace Hardware
acehardware.com
Dowels, brass strip wire, washers, and other hardware

More Ways to Enjoy Wirework!

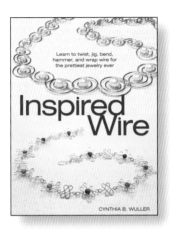

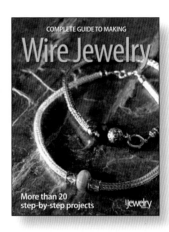

Inspired Wire guides wireworkers of all levels through a personal journey of design and creativity. Clear instructions, a unique building-block approach to basics, step-by-step photographs, and an eight-page gallery of the author's work make this book a stunning addition to any jewelry maker's collection. 36 projects in all.
62564 • 112pgs • $21.95

Twenty-one projects show you how to combine wireworking skills with beaded jewelry design. The projects use a wide variety of beads and cabochons, giving you plenty of opportunities to explore your creativity and expand your wireworking skills.
62649 • 112pgs • $21.95

This all-new collection features projects that move from the basics to a comfortable challenge of increasing complexity. The fresh, fashionable ideas include a mix of metals (copper, bronze, silver) and introduce exciting elements (rivets, metal blanks) and new tools (dapping block, hole-punching pliers).
64186 • 112pgs • $21.95

More than 20 exciting projects from *Art Jewelry* magazine introduce fundamental wireworking techniques, including wrapping, coiling, weaving, chain mail, cold connections, and soldering. Shape wire into beautiful necklaces, earrings, bracelets, rings, and more!
62540 • 112pgs • $21.95

P13614